RAMBLINGS
from the
SHOWER

Dottie,
To one who
truly understands!
I love you!
Faye
Galatians 1:10 NLT

INTEGRITY,
FAITH AND OTHER
SIMPLE YET
SLIPPERY ISSUES

FAYE BRYANT

ISBN: 1-4392-4032-9
ISBN-13: 9781439240328
Library of Congress Control Number: 2009904423

Visit www.booksurge.com to order additional copies.

No pithy dedication here. Simply that my heart longs for those who read these words to benefit from them.

Please move along. Don't forget to cap the shampoo and put the soap back in the dish.

Disclaimer:

The author is not a theologian, nor a doctor of psychology, nor an expert in any field other than her own life.

CONTENTS

Ramblings from the Shower

...discussions with God. · 1

People Pedestals and Potato Soup

...impossible expectations. · 7

Living

...truly living life. · 13

Letting Go

...grief. · 31

Lessons From a Little Dog

...excitement and surrender. · 35

Be Who You Be

...integrity. · 41

It Just Doesn't Matter

...judging and being judged. · 55

Up? Down? Run Around?

...a wrong way to worship? · 63

Heartbeat of God
...*pleasing God.* · 73

Jonah Trips
...*obedience and consequences.* · 87

Finding Fruit
...*patience, self-control, kindness, and others.* · · · · · · · · · · · · · · · 99

God Laughs
...*humor and sarcasm.* · 103

This is Good?
...*understanding His thoughts.* · 111

Healing
...*God's sovereignty.* · 119

Sticks and Stones
...*abusive relationships.* · 131

No Cover-ups
...*admitting mistakes.* · 145

Don't Wait
...*apologies.* · 155

You Can't Make Me Mad
...*control. Who gets it?* · 159

God Loves a Smart-Alec

...*being real.* · 173

Conversations with a Cynic

...*answering well.* · 179

Get a Clue!

...*why the heck are you here?* · 189

Tying the Bow

...*bringing it all together.* · 193

Acknowledgements

· *197*

Ramblings
from the Shower

...discussions with God.

Sometimes God shows up to share answers with us in the strangest places. Sometimes it's in a quiet morning place where one sips coffee and reads the Bible. Sometimes it is in the middle of a sermon in church. Many times for me, it is in the shower.

Have you ever thought about what you do in the shower . . . besides the obvious? I mean, shampoo, condition, soap, rinse—it's all pretty automatic. So what *else* do you do while in the shower?

My confession: I talk in the shower. No, I didn't say sing, I said talk. I guess it's more of a rambling stream of consciousness. In reality, that's where this book was born. Having grown up as an only child, I've grown quite accustomed to talking things through with myself. Funny thing about that is I never had any imaginary friends, but I did talk to myself a lot. Still do.

Nowadays I tend to see this conversation less with myself and more with God—prayer time. I find myself just going on and on with a God-conversation. Sometimes it's out loud; sometimes it is silent. Sometimes it is when I'm walking in the parking lot of Walmart, and sometimes it's in the shower. Therein lies the premise for the writings into which you are about to delve.

Most of these conversations with God have started with me asking Him questions during my quiet time, whether it is something I don't understand in the Bible or in my life or in the world, and then talking it through in the shower. Sometimes the radio is on and that just adds to the conversation. Listening to news and talk radio is fuel for my ramblings.

We live in a time when we hear left and right about people doing so many unethical things and so many immoral things. I don't know why integrity seems so simple to me or why just making a right choice seems so hard for some people. I can remember back in middle school—don't ask how long ago *that* was—we were required to memorize the poem "If" by Rudyard Kipling:

> If you can keep your head when all about you
>
> Are losing theirs and blaming it on you,
>
> If you can trust yourself when all men doubt you
>
> But make allowance for their doubting too,
>
> If you can wait and not be tired by waiting,

Or being lied about, don't deal in lies,

Or being hated, don't give way to hating,

And yet don't look too good, nor talk too wise:

If you can dream—and not make dreams your master,

If you can think—and not make thoughts your aim;

If you can meet with Triumph and Disaster

And treat those two impostors just the same;

If you can bear to hear the truth you've spoken

Twisted by knaves to make a trap for fools,

Or watch the things you gave your life to, broken,

And stoop and build 'em up with worn-out tools:

If you can make one heap of all your winnings

And risk it all on one turn of pitch-and-toss,

And lose, and start again at your beginnings

And never breathe a word about your loss;

If you can force your heart and nerve and sinew

To serve your turn long after they are gone,

And so hold on when there is nothing in you

Except the Will which says to them: "Hold on!"

If you can talk with crowds and keep your virtue,

Or walk with kings—nor lose the common touch,

If neither foes nor loving friends can hurt you;

If all men count with you, but none too much,

If you can fill the unforgiving minute

With sixty seconds' worth of distance run,

Yours is the Earth and everything that's in it,

And—which is more—you'll be a Man, my son!

Back when I originally read this, it was a list of lofty goals that a person might possibly—maybe on a good day—attain. Besides, it was for boys, not me. Try as I might, I knew I would never be a man, and I was okay with that.

Now as I read it, I realize that so much of what Kipling said actually speaks to mature adulthood, not just to the male gender. I find that much of what I've learned in my life is written right there in that poem. I do have perhaps more of a Biblical viewpoint on some of this, but the simplicity has always amazed me.

So now you know. The thoughts started there, under the running water. From there, study began, and the words have now found their way to paper. It is my sincere hope that you not only enjoy these thoughts, but that the words and ideas make a difference in your life and to those around you.

Perhaps Kipling's poem partially formed these random musings. May they challenge you to consider who you are and who you want to be. My desire is that, in your pondering, you will discover God and His thoughts about you and for you and His amazing plans for your life.

You will see that each chapter opens with the question that sparked the conversation. Maybe you've asked some of these very questions. Maybe my conclusions will help you in your search for an answer.

PEOPLE PEDESTALS AND POTATO SOUP

...impossible expectations.

*Lord, it's so hard sometimes to be a servant in Your
ministry when people put us up on pedestals from
which we will undoubtedly fall. What do we do?*

The music minister's wife was quite large and uncomfortably pregnant with their second child. By this time she was unable to even lie down at night to sleep. Yet she came to church to step up into the choir loft to sing, because her husband was the music minister, and it wouldn't look right if she wasn't there.

The pastor was worn out because it was his job to visit all the shut-ins at their homes, those in the hospitals and nursing homes, teach a Sunday School class, and preach three sermons a week, never mind his family obligations.

James does tell us in chapter 3 that we who hold a position as a teacher of Scripture will be held to a higher standard by God. However, it seems that the people in churches hold their pastors, staff, deacons, and respective spouses in this higher regard and expectation as if they, the good church folk, are God with the right to set the standards and the right to judge based on those standards. Sometimes they expect those in any form of leadership position to be superhuman and super-spiritual. They put them on a pedestal as someone to point out as an example of perfection. The problem with that is the only one perfect enough to be held up as an example is Jesus, and the only way off one of those pedestals, in most cases, is to fall. That's when the pointing as an example becomes malicious and judgmental.

Case in point, a good friend of mine has been a pastor's wife for about twenty years. Throughout that time she has been compelled to host certain parties, dress a certain way, and wear a certain hairstyle, in addition to answering for going on vacation and for why her children weren't perfect. She's been expected to know when anyone in the church, or a member of their family, was in the hospital or sick at home, and at least visit that person and prepare a meal to deliver to them.

Being a woman of grace and mercy, she took on all those roles and valiantly tried to be everything everyone wanted her to be, almost to the point of total burnout. Over the years, her husband has gone through his own experience of near burnout, landing himself in the emergency room with a grossly elevated blood pressure.

Not very long ago, this pastor's wife was doing all she could in a fairly new church plant, serving as the leader in two very important ministries as well as being the pastor's wife. The day came when a member's relative was in the hospital, and the member was spending hours each day with that relative. While the member did not communicate the need for company at the hospital or relief from a position in one of those ministries, she expected both the pastor and his wife to know those very things that were not communicated.

One day, in her role of a ministry leader, the pastor's wife made the mistake of calling this member for information regarding her part in that ministry.

WHAM!

BAM!

ZOWIE!

And the fall thereof was great.

The member was devastated that the pastor's wife had not noticed the long days that she was spending at the hospital tending to the sick relative and even had the nerve to ask for something related to the ministry that the member had been unable to prepare. The pastor's wife had fallen from that place on her pedestal into an inescapable mire. The member's devastation turned to anger, which grew into bitterness. Although reconciliation was sought and forgiveness was spoken, the heart remained bitter and hard, and the friendship and membership were abandoned.

This pastor's wife has survived many such falls off her unwanted pedestal over the years and has only recently taken the stand of refusing to step back up on it, in part because of some potato soup.

This one began with me. I spent a week very sick with pneumonia. The pastor's wife offered to prepare and deliver her famous potato soup for my husband and me on that Friday night. I tried to talk her out of it, but she insisted it was no trouble, so I agreed. Six o'clock came, and around seven, I got an e-mail from the pastor saying that his wife had spent the day taking her sons to various doctors for some fairly serious issues and had forgotten the soup until I had called to find out when she was going to bring it. Though I had told her not to worry about it, he had come home to find her weeping as she furiously scrubbed five pounds of potatoes for the soup. He managed to get her calmed down then sent the message to me.

Allow me to digress a moment. Some time ago, when I first took on a ministry role, a dear friend and mentor pointed out to me this problem of remaining on the pedestals upon which people place us. I was trying to meet expectations of others that ultimately failed and created stress and havoc in my own life and home. She took me through scripture to show me God's plan for priorities in my life.

The first is easy. You will have no other gods before the Lord God.

The second is not as obvious, yet in reality it is. The second relationship or institution, if you will, that God created was marriage. It would stand to reason that He counts this union as extremely important as well as the fruit of that relationship, our children. It seems from the Ten Commandments to Ephesians 6 that God places great value on the relationship with parents, too. Boil that all down to our second priority being family—marriage first, children second, and extended family third.

This places the church and ministry behind the other two. There are those who would debate this, saying that the call of God on one's life takes top priority. I believe He knows us well enough to know our spouse, children, and other family matters when He calls us. I also believe that He instituted those things, and our service to Him will enhance them rather than take away from them.

It was these words that I shared with my broken-hearted friend. She was so sure that she would receive the scars to match those from previous falls that her tears flowed easily, until both my husband and I assured her that we would not starve to death, nor would we even go hungry.

We both believed that her place that day had been with a son dealing with a badly injured foot and the other having a cyst on his back tended to, not in the kitchen preparing a meal for us.

I'm not sure which of us learned more from that Great Potato Soup Escapade. I think we all learned that pedestals don't work for anyone. Regardless of their height, they are far too wobbly and dangerous to attempt standing on.

The hard part comes when I want to put someone else on a pedestal. I have to remind myself that pastor or that leader or even that friend is not and cannot be all that I need from them. Only God can fill that role all the time. So here is a declaration: while I might admire you, enjoy your company, or think you are the cat's meow, I won't be putting your feet up on a pedestal. I'd rather have you right down here with me so that we can help each other along life's way. Deal?

I'm very proud of my friend, the pastor's wife. She's learned how to gracefully extricate herself from the pedestals people try to place her on. She has blossomed into a beautiful, fallible mess, given wholly over to God to be used for His glory.

Oh, and by the way, we finally got the soup on Sunday, and it was absolutely wonderful.

LIVING

...truly living life.

*Lord, I've never known anyone like Rich, who loved even
as a teen and now loves and trusts You so completely in
this season of his life when his body is dying. Where
does that come from? How can I get to that place?*

I've struggled with an incorrect self-image for most of my life.
In high school I was definitely not in the "cool" crowd. Matter of
fact, try as I might, I can't recall very many people from high school
who bothered knowing me, and I don't remember anyone wanting
to spend time with me. Whether that's true or not, it's what I
remember.

Funny how God always puts an "however" person in your life
though. My "however" person was Rich Willis. He was definitely
one of the "cool" kids. Rich was the kind of guy who was involved
in everything. He was in band, which is where I met him. He also
worked on the yearbook and carried an astonishing grade point
average. He was a talented artist, which is where the "however"
came to be.

Rich was known for drawing fun caricatures of people in their yearbooks. They were never demeaning, only a fun take on the person as he knew them. I handed Rich my yearbook and asked him to write something in mine. I had saved an entire page just for his work, in case he needed the space. He was usually able to return the book after a period of class, but told me he would have to take it home for the night. I have to say, I was a bit concerned, not really sure how he saw me or what he might draw and write.

The next day, Rich handed my yearbook back to me. I saw the drawing of a hand mirror, complete with the reflective part, with some truly encouraging words. While the words made me smile at the time, mainly in disbelief, the effect of them was not to be known for several years. Through many moves from one city to another, that yearbook has never been misplaced, never lost. The thought that one page contained was a priceless treasure to me. The words there took me back to a place where someone believed in me as someone worth knowing, instead of the words I was hearing each day that said quite the opposite.

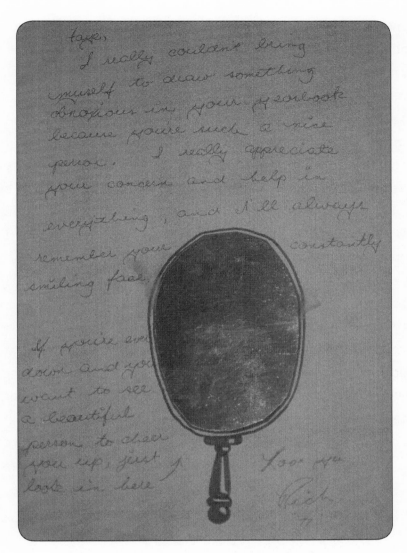

The caricature Rich drew in my yearbook, 1976.

In January 2009, after thirty-two years, I was able to reconnect with Rich. I learned about his life over the years, that he had at one point actually lived and worked in the same county where I now live. I learned that he was married, and they have two children, one in college and the other in middle school. It was a special thing to be able to remind him of what he had written to me and to tell him that it had really gotten me through some tough times.

I also learned that in 2007 he was diagnosed with cancer and has been dealing with it ever since. In late May 2009, Rich was told to "get things in order." In true "Rich" fashion, he questioned exactly what that meant—Did that mean twelve weeks from the date of that conversation and if he gets some medicinal help that adds a few weeks? Does that mean it is added on to the twelve? Let me just show you his words:

June 9, 2009:

I'm curious. Are Doctors just really bad with calendar dates? 'Cause when he said to me and Connie "This is finally that conversation I never want to have with a patient" I of course asked, "Okay, izzat three weeks? Six weeks? Three months?" he just said, "I'd take my summer trips earlier, rather than later." No wonder you can never find these guys on a Friday afternoon, and I'll bet it's not that they're all out on the golf course. It's probably that the rest of the office staff wants that afternoon off every week, and they figure the doctor won't notice if they don't schedule him in, because he really is that bad with DATES and TIMES!

That's my guess, anyway. So, tell me, when your doctor kinda gave you that squiggly sorta, "I might put it somewhere between three and six or eight weeks or so, if things don't change" speech, what did you do? Well, of course, what I did was I thought to myself, "okay, what are you fixing to change?" It's all right, my mind kinda works that way...

So now, just to mess up my schedule more, we've added a whole chemo regimen on top of the holding pattern chemo I was on, and then we're going to be adding focused radiation therapy to one lung or the other to see if that will slow things down. That's fine, and I'm all for it, and at this point, I guess I'm for whatever else is in the kitchen that he thinks he wants to throw in the mixer. The question is, of course, if it helps a teeny bit, do I get to add it to the six-week date, or do I have to take it at the end of the shorter three week schedule?

Do you see my predicament? Sheesh, how do you plan for dinner a week from Thursday?

When people hear all of this, then come the suggestions from well meaning types. I know you've heard a couple of songs suggested, or even played at someone's memorial or funeral, like "Live like you were Dyin'," or "One Life to Love" or something like that, right? I think before anyone else makes a suggestion like that they should go back and listen to the lyrics carefully for once. What I notice about these two songs in particular is that they seem to point to people's tendencies to put things off until there's no time left. I'm trying to think how that suggestion might have any application to me? Ummm, nope, nothing coming to mind. I've kinda been doing what I always wanted to do as soon as the opportunity made itself available. Is there anything I feel I need to get done yet? Well, there still is a long prayer list with people who are in need - that's still a priority. Did I go skydiving because I figured I needed to do it before I died? No, I jumped out of an airplane because I got a job at a place that makes GREAT parachutes, I made friends with a GREAT Tandem instructor named Tom Noonan, and Tom said one day, "Let's go jumping this weekend!" If you are ready to do things when God provides you with the opportunity, then you get to go do things. Things that God has not provided an opportunity for me to do, I really have no plans of trying to get done.

I'll try to be plain and clear, here. My heart could stop beating tonight. Yours could too. So if a doctor tells me that I might not be around to carve pumpkins this year, do you really think that I'm going to do anything different than I have been? Only people who live life unprepared would do things that way. Consider carefully what I am trying to communicate to you here. I'll bet MOST people who die in this country won't get a six-week notice. That's not ME. That's all of YOU.

Plus, who knows, maybe the cancer will only respond to the kitchen sink treatment. We haven't tried it all yet, so who knows?

Okay, I'll admit it. I would like to finish cleaning out the garage. But that's it.

So, this week we are getting oxygen supplies and tank durations sorted out, trying to get the scooter thing put together and waiting on a radiation schedule. Then it's back to bothering doctors and nurses, hopefully working a little, and complimenting young ladies and gentlemen when they play nice and hold the door open for old guys wearing Hawaiian shirts pushing oxygen tanks around. Sometimes the ones who don't bother to hold the door accidentally get bumped on the heel by the oxygen tank.

Sorry. It makes me smile. [1]

————————————————

There you see a brief view into the heart of this man I feel honored to have counted as a friend.

In late May 2009, I shared with Rich that my husband, Jack, and I were planning a trip to Kissimmee after Christmas. He told me that the way things were looking he wouldn't be around at Christmas.

[1] Link to Rich's CancerBlog here: http://web.me.com/richwillis/CancerBlog/Home_Base.html Medical Update #59

That set up the opportunity of *two* lifetimes. My husband and I traveled with another friend to visit with Rich and his wife one Saturday morning in mid-June. We were able to sit together with other friends, lingering over breakfast at Cracker Barrel for two hours before his strength was gone. What a wonderful two hours!

The one thing that I came away from that brief time with him was that though this man's body was dying, *he was not.*

Rich's body was ravaged by disease, but his mind and his heart were fixed on the good things. He lived as an example of the verses in Philippians: "And now, dear brothers and sisters, one final thing. Fix your thoughts on what is true, and honorable, and right, and pure, and lovely, and admirable. Think about things that are excellent and worthy of praise. Keep putting into practice all you learned and received from me—everything you heard from me and saw me doing. Then the God of peace will be with you" (Philippians 4:8-9 NLT).

In the week before we met with Rich and his wife, he spent time—while sitting in his wheelchair— guiding his son through transforming a bicycle into a moped, including taking pictures and writing about it.

How does one get to that place where his or her faith is so solid that nothing, not even cancer, shakes it? Perhaps the better question would be how to get to that place ourselves, now?

I had written to Rich to get him to answer that question, but the day I sent it was the day he went into the hospital for his final stay there. Just a couple days later, he left. First he left the hospital, and then he left this life. So we will just have to dissect and disseminate to learn the answers, which, really, I believe will take the rest of our lives to truly grasp. Rich decided a long time ago Who he was going to believe in. He placed his faith firmly and squarely in God, believing that God is everything He said He is, perfect in every way and utterly sovereign. Once that decision was out of the way, the rest, as they say, was gravy.

Believing that God had ordained his life and given him every provision for living it, Rich lived. He studied hard, learning new things up till the very end. He married a beautiful woman with whom he shared love and ideals and passions. He constantly looked for challenges. And within all that, he saw God. He believed that in every instance, God orchestrated the details.

I'm there, I think. I love looking at situations and realizing that even when I thought that I was the one making a decision, I learn that in reality God was guiding my every step, working out details that I never even knew existed. The difference is, many times, I don't realize that until after all was said and done. I think Rich learned the fine art of seeing God's hand in the midst of the uncertainties of life and realizing that fact made the uncertain quite certain.

So there is no real answer *per se*, only faith. Believing that even when you don't see God's hand in the midst of your uncertainties,

He is still there working things out for good. I believe that even when Rich was a teen, drawing caricatures in high school yearbooks, he felt God guiding his hand and his heart to put the right thing on the page. I believe that when Rich chose a college, a career, a wife, a home, and all that goes with living, he felt God guiding every decision; and he gratefully left the details, both large and small, to the Creator.

Here's the thing that some of us miss, though: many of us believe that way, but Rich lived it—day in and day out where people could see it. Perhaps this challenge of living the past two years with cancer brought it to the forefront, because people tend to pay more attention when we're battling horrible enemies.

Rich had good days and bad days. I learned about that at the breakfast table, listening to his wife share from her heart. He had ups and downs. He was just like the rest of us. Yet even in the midst of the bad, he looked for the *good*. He knew that God was there, perhaps unseen and unfelt, but there nonetheless; and he lived his life based on that fact. Again, a few words from the man himself on April 15, 2009:

———————————

Timing, Focus, Goals and Success, or what you can learn from Cancer treatment, sometimes.

While I've been sitting around, getting my chemo, taking a break from chemo, feeling yucky, feeling great, and working as much as I can, (huff, puff), and finally getting back on chemo, my good friend Clay has completed the final draft of his first (as far as he's told me) screenplay, has sent it off to Hollywood, and having had the honor of proofreading the project, I have some confidence that you are likely to see this on the 'Big Screen' before too long. It's a good piece of writing, and it sounds like Clay has made some good connections, so I think for him, anything is possible.

My friend Michelle is also on a good path. She recently decided to put her thoughts into book form, and she is always thinking in stories. I haven't read her latest draft, but I have been reading both of her blogs (she writes nice things about me), and I think she is going to do very well as a writer. She has made some really good connections in the feature animation community, so whether it's novels, story books or writing for TV, she seems to be on the right path, as well.

Michelle met another friend of mine (who has also written nicely about me) this week in Knoxville, Faye. No doubt Fay and Michelle were quite entertaining to each other at my expense. Faye has her book on its way to being published, and I really look forward to reading the first copy (you'll send it to me, right Faye?) to see the results of all of her hard work.

Gentry, another friend from way back, decided that he wanted to become a Jazz Singer, and at 54, he jumped headlong into it. This month (next week, actually) he'll be performing with some other jazz musicians of note in public, in Rhode Island.

I'm going to mention one more person, Chase, who's a little different than the other friends mentioned earlier, because everyone I know who knows him and Suzie, already thought of him as a success. A brilliant show producer at Disney, we collectively wondered what he would be able to do next. This past year, however, Chase wrote and produced an Anglicized version of a popular Chinese stage show, which opened to rave reviews on Broadway in New York.

What all of these friends of mine have in common, and the reason they come to mind when I think of success, is that their quest for new successes began in their 40's or 50's. Each one of these individuals has had unusual odds stacked against them, in one way or another, though I won't mention them specifically. Please trust me when I tell you that most people would have given up simply from the magnitude of the challenges these folks have had earlier in their lives. Guess which of my friends I can say truly inspire me? Yup, listed above.

That's not to say that I'm not inspired by other friends or acquaintances, but I do have a point I want to make, and these I've mentioned fit my lesson perfectly. Now let me defend my credentials just a tiny bit, so that you understand why I am impressed by this notable few. I have worked as a still photographer for Walt Disney World, done work for popular television shows, worked in short and feature films, and done video production with and for some people who's names you've no doubt seen near the beginning of film credits at the theatre. I have been a stage performer, and a movie producer. I have watched and worked with people who worked tirelessly for years towards a goal to achieve it, and I have worked with many others who worked just as hard, for just as long, only to attend their funerals before they reached their goal. I've been around a bit. I think my opinion carries a little weight. I've seen plenty of "almost" talent. These people, in my opinion, have "The Right Stuff."

Now here's the lesson- or at least the question...

Are you successful? Am I? Are you trying to be? Do you want to be? I'm a bit jaded on my own behalf, I must admit. The CV on my website doesn't begin to cover it all. If I listed all of my wins, my awards, my individual successes, you'd think I was boasting, or in some cases, gloating. But do you know, or can you guess, what I consider all of that to be? If you guessed, "Interesting conversation topics at reunions" you'd be right. As each one of my accomplishments of the past came into my grasp, I would think, "This is GREAT! How could it get any better?"

But it DID!

I would anguish over what to do next, where to set my next goal or target. Sometimes, when I couldn't see the path, I'd get downright low, nearly depressed. But none of the successes that followed ever seemed to have a connection with the one before, so it became impossible to really set a new goal. Frustrating.

Hindsight is a remarkable thing. Clearly the things I seem to have accomplished by myself were provided to me through God's providence. I don't know exactly when that hit me, but it was really a long time ago, maybe the day I married Connie. What a gift from God! The realization, from looking back, that it was God's guidance that had set all of my accomplishments up made me realize that I didn't need to worry about finding my next target, for God was already leading me there, if only I didn't get stupid and wander off his path. The original accomplishments might have been relatively insignificant, Youth Orchestra, Track victories, Yearbook recognition, scholarships, Solo Trombonist in the College Jazz Ensemble, promotions at work, professional studio work, private pilot license, you name it, each one was a little better than the one before. God has truly blessed me. But only to teach me, I think.

I don't worry about what's coming next. God is in control. It's a choice- you either let him shoulder the load, or you carry it all yourself, including the planning, the hoping, the waiting, and the disappointment if it doesn't work out this time: Yours---By yourself---All Alone---All Yours, even if you think your friends are enough to help you with it. I have always had friends, close friends, it seems, but even so, I haven't always been happy or felt encouraged. But God NEVER leaves you. And just as you can believe my observations that these friends have gone through tough obstacles and persevered, you can believe that I can see God's handiwork in looking back on my life so far.

So this cancer thing shows up. Gee, what kind of accomplishment is THAT? Well ponder what I have been sharing with you, that I'm on a path God put me on, and nobody really knows my next target, because not even I know what that is. And does this drive me crazy? Some people already think that I am. It can be rationally explained though, if you understand that I am never worried, because not only do I know, but I understand that God is in charge. And I am patient, not because I have studied and practiced and learned patience, but because I know, and I understand that God works on his own schedule, and his schedule will accomplish more in my life than my own schedule will.

Cancer, and its treatment, is a thing. Just a THING! It would be silly and illogical to worry about a thing that you have absolutely no control over. My Doctor, and my nurses, aren't in control of my situation. It's kinda sad, really, to think about. A surgeon has control over the operating room, in that he can choose a tool that has been tested and proven to work, his skills with his tools are the result of lots of practice, and barring all of those little things that could happen, he can generally predict what the outcome will be. But an Oncologist is an educated guesser. He relies, of course, on years of training, and on constant reviews of current medical news and trials and their outcomes, but no one can tell whether the treatment chosen will cure you, or kill you, or, as it seems to be in my case, simply keeping things from growing out of control. After my last CAT scan and bloodwork review, Dr. A. informed me of some new concerns: One of the larger nodules in my lungs is beginning to press against an artery, and could eventually close that blood vessel off. Of more significance, though, my CEA, or Cancer Marker results show an increase from around 7 to almost 90, whatever those numbers mean. All I know is one is higher than the other, and the Doctor seemed to be very concerned about that. Oh, yeah, then there's the super duper high blood pressure. I think my body is just doing that to exercise my capillaries so I won't have an unexpected blowout someday. So he's suggested that I get rolling on enrollment in a clinical trial very soon. Expeditiously, you might say, with haste even.

I know, it sounds like, "Hey, kid, I've done all I can do for you, your only chance now is experimental drug therapy." Well you may have been watching too many medical dramas on TV. Not that you are wrong, but you may truly be watching too much TV. What he kinda said was, "Hey, kid, I've done all I can do for you, your only chance now is clinical trials." I met with the head of the Colon Cancer Oncology department at USC in California about two years ago. He told me then that they always had some sort of trial going on, and it was generally pretty easy to get scheduled into one, so I have put my brother the Doctor on notice that he may soon have a roommate. Connie will love it, I'm sure, with lots of quiet time, and only Trek to clean up after. (Don't worry, honey, I'll call you every half-hour to keep you up to date, you know, like John and Sandy?). I hope she'll miss me just a little, but realistically it's just another thing, right? Something else to be accomplished. And success with this dance I'm having with my condition, however you measure it, has already been assured, because of the one who is really in charge of my life, and who is responsible for all of my past successes.

How long until I leave? How long will treatment last? How long until I come back home? How long do I have?

You know those answers as well as I do - who can tell? The only thing I know to do is to rely on the successes of my friends above. It doesn't matter how long it takes, if you are working towards the right goal or goals. These friends were all in their forties and fifties before they LOOKED for a new goal, and they've all already achieved it. Think of all the people who have been chasing a dream for forty or fifty years, and haven't reached it yet, or who only recently have! Are they successful? They are if their goal is set before them by the right guide. You know who I mean...

"...so grow you not weary in well doing, for in the end you shall reap, if you faint not." -Gal 6:9

So there you have it. If your goals are taking a really long time to produce fruit, choose to be patient. Give God time to make it work out for you. If you are struggling with the load you are carrying along the way, maybe you should consider changing your focus, not your goal. Give Him a chance to help you.

I started chemo again today, but my focus tonight is to get all the way through my prayer list, which seems to grow every week. I'm praying for all of you. Do I feel successful, myself? I never really have thought about it. My goal is to see what God will succeed at through me. In all appropriate humility.[2]

Not much more that I can say. My hope is that if you haven't been doing so before, that you begin now.

Live!

---

2   Rich's blog, Medical Update #55

LETTING GO

...grief.

God, it is so hard to lose someone. I've experienced
the loss of people I love to divorce, death, and the
end of a friendship. Why does it hurt so much?
What can I do about it? How long does it take?

Grief affects us all at one time or another. Even Jesus experienced grief. He cried when he was faced with the reality of the death of his good friend Lazarus (John 11:35). Why should we think we would react any differently?

I think most of us know we'll cry over the loss. The thing is, we live in what I call a "microwave" or "Twitter" society now. We expect the pain to be gone in moments. We expect to express our anguish in 140 characters or less. Oddly enough, it just doesn't work that way.

If you've ever watched the epic movie *Gone with the Wind*, you've seen the part where Scarlett's first husband was killed in a battle, and she appears at a fundraising ball wearing black. She is faithfully attending to a concession booth, because dancing wasn't expected of any widow. (Of course, only Rhett knew that she wasn't really grieving.) Back then, a widow was expected to grieve for at least a year. That meant she wasn't expected to be "normal" in any way. She wasn't expected to be the life of any party. She wasn't expected to keep from crying when she saw something that reminded her of her loss. She wasn't expected to just move on. She was expected to grieve, to work through the feelings and sensations of the enormous loss in her life. She was expected to take time out for this event in her life, and then ease back into society. (Okay, I know that in the movie it was no great loss to Scarlett, but we're talking about the expectations of society, not her in particular.)

Today we expect to have the funeral on Friday and be back at work on Monday. We expect people to just keep doing what they've always done. It doesn't matter if their world has been turned upside down. It doesn't matter if that person has to think through everything they do, including taking that next breath. It's that microwave mentality. Ding! You're done.

Just as bad, we don't think that all loss is loss. I mean, just because a friend you spent four out of seven days every week with no longer speaks to you, that's not a loss you need to grieve, is it? Just because you are divorced, that's not like a real death, right? Experience either one, and then tell your heart and mind that those aren't losses or that they aren't deaths.

Every grief sets off a series of stages. Psychologists a lot smarter than I am say there are seven stages of grief, and some of us may go through them numerous times before we can say we are done.

The main thing about grief that I see is that we need to give ourselves a couple of things. The first is time. We may have to go back to work and church, but when we go home, we can give ourselves the gift of time. We can spend time thinking about that person and all they've meant to us. We can relive the memories and enjoy the moments.

The second is emotions. We cannot be afraid of them. We are angry. We are sad. We feel lost and alone. We are afraid. God knows all that. Jesus has felt all that. Tell Him. Sometimes you will want to tell Him at the top of your lungs. Go ahead, He can handle it.

Those who are friends with someone who has suffered loss have an incredible chance to show love and compassion. Many times, however, we want to fix our friend's pain. I hate to tell you this, but that's not gonna happen. You are not God. Relax. Just sit with that friend. You don't have to say anything. Keep an eye on them and make sure they're not sinking into utter despair. Make sure they eat once in a while. Be there. Your loving presence will speak more healing into their life than your words ever could. And don't expect them to be "normal" again for a while. That's okay. Remember the old days. They weren't all that bad.

Lessons From a Little Dog

...excitement and surrender.

It is so funny to watch Casey's ears perk up when he hears the truck. It's like he knows that's the one that belongs here. Then watching him roll over or bounce on his hind legs until he's noticed, it makes me laugh every time!

Many of you will be able to relate to these lessons, but how many times do we apply them? Act on them?

Casey is our eleven-year-old toy poodle. Some would think it strange to say that a little dog could teach a great spiritual lesson, but isn't it about how we view the actions and attitudes of others as to what kind of lesson we learn from them?

We acquired Casey as a puppy shortly before my husband had back surgery. The original idea was that he would be my dog. I had owned a miniature poodle when I was a teen and loved him so much that we thought this would be a great match. Well that six-week recuperation time, when my husband was home alone with him, cemented into Casey's little doggie brain exactly who his master is—and *he* isn't me! (Although I *have* become the vice-master.)

We've all heard stories (can anyone remember Marlin Perkins and the *Mutual of Omaha's Animal Kingdom*?) about how keen a dog's hearing is. What we hear less often is just how smart they can be.

Casey has learned the sound of each of the motors in our three automobiles along with the sound of those vehicles' doors closing.

If he's not completely lost in his afternoon nap in the sun, he will hear the arrival of his master. His response is to jump up and down, many times on only two legs, as he proceeds toward the front door. He will voice his excitement in whimpers, woofs, and barks. He will run to the door, then back to me, and then to the door again as if to say, "He's here! Open the door! He's here! Let him in!" Then when the door is opened and he is reunited with his master, he wiggles and snuffles and woofs and sits and wiggles and pants and watches until his master notices him and speaks to him. His joy is complete only when the master sits and beckons Casey into his lap.

Isn't that a glorious picture of how we should be? I mean, I know God's everywhere all the time, but do we get excited about going in to a quiet place to spend time with Him? Do we approach our Heavenly Father with joyful expectation? Not of what He can do for us and the blessings He will give, but a joyful expectation of simply being in His presence? Do we ever long for, with whimpers, wiggles, and cries, the touch of His hand or the sound of His voice? The chance to sit in His lap and bask in His presence? I want to get to that place.

Another thing Casey does, when his master draws near to him, he rolls over in utter surrender.

Chew on that one for a minute. (Pardon the pun.)

Picture yourself—juggling your to-do list, controlling family schedules, work schedules, and church schedules, when you realize He's right there.

He's reaching down to you.

Will you let go?

Will you drop the calendar? The notes? The ideas and plans—the control—to open yourself up fully in complete surrender?

That doesn't mean you have to stop doing. That means you change . . . your mindset.

Instead of your objectives, you look for His—God's.

Instead of you being the driving force in your job, your family, your life, God is.

Control. We all love to have it. We feel we must maintain it. But when it comes to living the way God wants us to, we have to let go of it completely. It is scary. It is frightening. It goes against every ounce of our human thinking. Yet it is only in that surrender that we realize full success.

When Casey rolls over, he ends up getting attention from his master. His belly gets a rub, and he experiences happiness.

When we give up control of our life, we get attention from our Master. The Creator of Universe takes time to show us Himself. We can experience His presence, and hear from Him.

What could be better?

So, let's try that. Next time you go to sit down and pray or read your Bible, have a "quiet time," or whatever you want to call it; try thinking like Casey.

God's here! Open the door!

He's here! Let Him in!

Imagine quivering with excitement, whimpering excitedly until He sits and invites you to join Him. Then just jump into His lap and feel His love envelope you. Hear the rumble of His voice as He tells you what He wants you to know. Hear Him reveal His heart to you. Hear Him share His plans for your life.

Oh, how amazing that is. And we have it. Every time we sit down and open the Bible, the Author, the Creator of Heaven and Earth meets us there.

Show your excitement. Open your heart and your arms. Surrender to the Master fully, and let Him shower you with His attention.

Be Who You Be

...integrity.

God, why do people lie and cheat, and then they're so surprised when people don't trust them? Why do people have such a hard time understanding what integrity is? Why don't they understand just how precious and tenuous it is? It seems so simple..."

Integrity. A word tossed around a lot, but what does it mean?

It means, "Be who you be."

When you look in the mirror, who do you see? Who is that person, right there, looking back at you? Is that your alter ego or your true self? Seriously, I bet you have a split personality. As a matter of fact, I'm sure of it. When you are sitting in the pew at church, you are a different you than the you in the mirror. And what about when you are sitting in traffic that isn't moving? Then when the traffic does begin to move and that little compact whips right in front of you, now which personality is seen? What about in the checkout line—more specifically the express lane—and the person in front of you has thirty items? What was that you said when the referee botched that call in the last minutes of the big game?

Are you thinking about yourself in different situations now? Do you find yourself saying and doing things you don't intend?

Why is that? What's the deal? Here's a clue: You are human. Even the Apostle Paul dealt with this. He struggled day in and day out with being a godly man, yet he is known as a man of integrity. How can that be? How can a person who makes mistakes and struggles with their faith be considered a person of integrity? Hear his heart from his letter to the Romans in chapter 7, verses 15 through 25 (NLT):

I don't really understand myself, for I want to do what is right, but I don't do it. Instead, I do what I hate. But if I know that what I am doing is wrong, this shows that I agree that the law is good. So I am not the one doing wrong; it is sin living in me that does it. And I know that nothing good lives in me, that is, in my sinful nature. I want to do what is right, but I can't. I want to do what is good, but I don't. I don't want to do what is wrong, but I do it anyway. But if I do what I don't want to do, I am not really the one doing wrong; it is sin living in me that does it. I have discovered this principle of life—that when I want to do what is right, I inevitably do what is wrong. I love God's law with all my heart. But there is another power within me that is at war with my mind. This power makes me a slave to the sin that is still within me. Oh, what a miserable person I am! Who will free me from this life that is dominated by sin and death? Thank God! The answer is in Jesus Christ our Lord. So you see how it is: In my mind I really want to obey God's law, but because of my sinful nature I am a slave to sin.

Simply put, they be who they be.

They are the same every day, regardless of the situation. They speak the truth, no matter the cost. They keep their word. They do what they say they will do, when they say they will do it.

Great, huh?

Simple.

Okay, we're done.

Whoa! What if you're not there? Suppose you haven't arrived yet? You say you want to know how to get there?

Simply put, you must be who you be. You make up your mind today. Determine and decide exactly how you will act in any given situation. Then be that—every time.

When your wife asks that inevitable question—"Does this dress make me look fat?"— then you tell her the truth. Should you be brutal? Not if you want to stay married! Tell her that you think she's gorgeous, and neither that dress, nor any other article of clothing can ever possibly change that. Of course, for her to accept that answer, you should have been telling her that you think she's gorgeous all along.

Ladies, if your husband asks you, "Honey, does this go together?" as he holds up one plaid item and one striped, you can't fall over laughing at his fashion sense. You should find out what he thinks of the outfit he's chosen, which part of it he likes the most, then help him find the things that work with that item. Make sure he knows that it is because he's the handsomest thing you've ever seen, and you want him to look the best possible.

So, how does this look in action? How do you get from where you are now to "being who you be?" First of all, you have to make a confession. Confession means agreeing with truth. There are people who already know you aren't who you pretend to be. They probably live with you. Some may work with you. They know. Now you have to admit it to yourself. You have to realize and understand that the person in the mirror may not be who others see.

You might even have to go make some apologies.

Ouch!

You might have to admit out loud to your spouse and kids that you realize you've been pretending. You might even have to ask them to forgive you. Do you have co-workers who know you're not all that? What about the friends who have seen your good, bad, and ugly? Might as well add them to the list to have a talk with; they might be surprised, but it won't be because you are breaking the news to them of your faults. It will be because you are admitting it to yourself and to them.

Before I go any further, though, if you've failed at this before, stop beating yourself up! So you don't know what it means to be a person of integrity—yet.

Now wait. If you've failed at walking in integrity, then you know what it is; you just didn't get it right. So you know what it means. You're learning. You've decided you are not happy with where you've been or where you are at this point. You're trying. Isn't that why you are still reading these words, rather than the fact that you're bored and need distraction and entertainment?

Without a doubt, integrity is lacking around us today. It has become increasingly normal to read about celebrities and politicians—and even people in ministry—who have lied about something, have been caught cheating on their spouse, or have been caught in some other sin. Then we watch them try to justify it. How are we to even know what integrity means?

The same way we learn about anything that pertains to character: We check out what God says.

Job 1:8 and 2:3 gives us a definition— blameless. A man of complete integrity is blameless in what he does; he fears God and stays away from evil. Now don't start with that, "Who decides what evil is?" That's in the Book, too.

Job 27:3–6 says integrity is a treasure to guard, to speak no evil, speak no lies, defend it, and maintain one's innocence.

Psalm 25:21 says integrity protects us.

Psalm 26 says integrity is the source and expression of the motives of the heart.

Psalm 111:7–8 says God's commands are true, trustworthy, and to be obeyed with integrity (honesty without compromise or corruption).

Psalm 119:1 says that living in integrity brings joy.

Proverbs 2:7 says that God shields those who walk in integrity and grants a treasure of common sense to the honest.

Proverbs 10:9 reminds us to walk safely and to not slip and fall.

Finally, Titus 2:7 tells us that integrity can be modeled, can be emulated, can be learned, and is shown by good works.

There you have it. To walk in integrity, God expects us to be honest, no matter what. We are to resist corruption and abhor compromise. Simple enough? Yeah, right.

That means you have to beware of the "it's justa" monster! It is a tiny little thing, quicker than a nanosecond, and it can ruin relationships, cost jobs, and destroy every ounce of your credibility.

"It's justa little white lie," or "It's justa little thing, the office has tons of them, and no one will miss it if I take it, so it's not really stealing"—tiny little steps that become miles of distance between you and God.

So have you seen this "it's justa" monster in yourself? Do you see now how easy it is to walk away from integrity? Are you ready and willing to do something about it?

Excellent!

Time to take some small steps.

When someone asks you a question, do not answer it with the next breath. Take a second and seek the honesty that lies within you—that comes from your Heavenly Father. Okay, now exhale and answer the question. Be honest, first with yourself, then with the other person.

Honestly share your heart and mind. Don't give the answer you think that person wants to hear, because if you do, you're not doing them, yourself, or your relationship any favors. But remember, we are told to tell the truth in love (Ephesians 4:15), so again, being brutal is wrong. So, as you think of your response, think about the delivery, too.

Why does the delivery matter? Because honesty is actually more than the spoken word. Sometimes it is actions. Sometimes it is beliefs. A person of integrity is honest through and through. Plus, if our words don't line up with our beliefs and actions then those things belie what we say.

An obvious example is the mother who tells her child not to smoke, telling him it is bad for him—just before she lights up.

A less evident example is the father who disciplines his child for lying, then leaves income off his Form 1040 at tax time, while asking himself, "Who will know?" The obvious and churchy answer is, "God knows," and He really does. It's not just a pat answer, it is truth. And beyond that, God cares about it, too. Lying is breaking one of the "Big Ten," you know.

What's that you say? We are not "under the Law" anymore? Yeah, I've heard that argument, too. The one that says that since Jesus came giving grace, we are no longer under the Law. We are no longer held to the Old Testament laws, including the Ten Commandments. Are you sure about that? Jesus' words in Matthew 5:17–18 seem to indicate that He intended for the Law to continue to guide our lives and actions:

Don't misunderstand why I have come. I did not come to abolish the law of Moses or the writings of the prophets. No, I came to accomplish their purpose. I tell you the truth, until heaven and earth disappear, not even the smallest detail of God's law will disappear until its purpose is achieved.

Jesus specifically said that he did not come to abolish the Law, but to accomplish it. The Merriam-Webster dictionary defines accomplish as, "To bring about (a result) by effort; to bring to completion: fulfill; to succeed in reaching." So, Jesus didn't come to do away with the Law, He came to bring about a result. Could it be that the result He wanted to accomplish was the change in our thinking—from doing something because it was a Law, to doing it because we love God and want to please Him? Could it be that He understood that a relationship would rule more effectively than written Law? Could this be why He made it possible for mankind to have a relationship with Him?

I think perhaps Jesus knew something else about the little things that we say "it's justa" about. There's that thing He always talked about—leaven. You know, yeast.

Yeast is cool. A batch of bread—two big steaming loaves—requires only a couple tablespoons of yeast. It gets all mixed in with the flour, milk, and sugar, and then makes them rise and grow. Then here's an amazing thing: You can punch it down, squish it, beat it back to a tiny size, and you know what?

It grows again—it doesn't stop.

That is the "little hidden lie," that "thing" that no one else sees or knows about. Yet, God knows, and you know. And worse yet, the enemy sees it. Then before you know it, you add a few hours on your timesheet. "It's justa little bit; I've worked hard for this company!" Next, you take an hour and a half for lunch, "It's justa few minutes, and it won't matter." Before long, you claim items in your workspace as "yours" even though they belong to your employer, "It's justa pen and some paper; it's no big deal."

How far do you let it grow before you decide to do something about it?

Jesus said something harsh in the Sermon on the Mount, right after he proclaimed all the "blesseds." He said, "You are the salt of the earth; but"—and here's the harsh part—"if the salt has become tasteless, how will it be made salty again? It is *good for nothing* anymore, except to be *thrown out and trampled underfoot* by men" (emphasis mine).

Let's see if I can 'splain it to you.

I don't know if you've ever lived on a farm—a few of you may have. I grew up a pseudo-country girl. Both my parents had grown up on farms, but we lived in Florida. I learned about raising a vegetable garden, particularly that if you don't water the radishes, they will get too hot to eat, but that's a whole 'nother story!

My husband is a farm boy, born and bred. He grew up milking cows, collecting eggs, plowing and harvesting, and lapping pines for fun. We tell people our second date was a hog killin'. Now, while that is somewhat true (it wasn't actually the second date), I should explain. This pseudo-country girl didn't have to endure the hard part of this process. What we, the collective family members, did that day was process the meat. The sides of the pork (half a hog) were brought in and cut to the desire of my father-in-law, after which he prepared each portion in various ways. Some of the meat was ground up with spices to become sausage. Tenderloins were sized into roasts or sliced for chops, and the hams were taken to the smokehouse to be cured.

Curing a country ham involves salt—a lot of salt and a salt box. The latter looks like a deep-drawer bureau. Its design was to allow salt to utterly surround the ham or bacon placed inside.

I'd read about this process, but as is the case so very often, living it was much more educational.

After a few weeks, it was time. Joy! Excitement! The first ham of the winter! (Picture my mouth watering here.)

I was excited again to be included, and accompanied this man I would later marry to the smokehouse to retrieve a ham. What a surprise greeted me when he had to literally break the block of salt that had formed around the meat. The loose grains we had poured into this drawer were now cemented together, forming an impenetrable layer around the ham. And get this, it wasn't salty, not like it had been!

Every ounce of the saltiness had gone into that which the salt was protecting from ruin—that which it was preserving. Now, the salt was just dropped on the dirt floor of an East Tennessee smokehouse, destined to be walked on as other items were retrieved.

What a picture! Do you see it? The salt was no longer salty, no longer of any use, and it was tossed aside and walked on. (Makes you think Jesus knew something about farm life, huh?)

We can get that way. Truly! Sometimes we get so busy pouring our lives, our saltiness, into the good things.

Family.

Friends.

Ministry.

Work.

However, if we pour all our saltiness into those things *without replenishing*, we become weak. Then in that weakened state, we find it so much easier to fall prey to the "it's justa" monster. The end result is we can't be or do the best that God has for us.

If we don't make the choice ahead of time to be utterly honest in every situation, in every circumstance, to resist corruption in every form, to abhor compromising truth and godliness, then we can and probably will fall away easily. Even when we think we're protecting and preserving something, we start being less and less salty. Then we are no longer good for anything. We are not good for teaching, leading, mentoring, or simply being a picture of someone worth knowing, much less a portrait of Christ.

Remember: God forgives. Get some more salt—spend time with Him in His Word, and replenish your saltiness. "It's justa" few minutes, and it will matter.

It Just Doesn't Matter

...judging and being judged.

God, why are people so amazed by the way our church just accepts them? Why does a person care so much more about how he or she looks when coming to church, as opposed to going to the grocery store?

There are many things that matter to God; many parts of your life are of great importance to Him. While it would be fairly easy to visit the list of things that do matter, I think we need to address some that do not.

When we use the phrase, "It just doesn't matter," in this instance, we are by no means saying that God doesn't care. Instead we are talking about His infinite love, His unconditional love for you—regardless of...anything.

Your race...just doesn't matter.

Your height and weight...just doesn't matter.

Your hair color, style, or lack thereof...just doesn't matter.

Compact, sedan, SUV, luxury, old, new, used, barely moving… just doesn't matter.

Suit and tie…just doesn't matter.

Dressy clothes at church…just doesn't matter.

Country, rock and roll, classical, jazz, gospel, contemporary Christian…it just does not matter.

You drink wine, beer, or liquor…it just doesn't matter.

You have lots of friends or none…nope, doesn't matter!

You're skinny, you're fat…doesn't matter.

You're athletic or a couch potato…just does not matter.

You're free, you're in jail…it really, truly doesn't matter.

Made some bad choices? Living in a lifestyle that isn't something God would like? It doesn't matter in reference to how much God loves you.

The thing is…God loves you, no matter where you are and what you've done or said or thought.

He loves you.

Period.

Forever.

All He requires of you is a broken and contrite heart. All He desires is your obedience. It does not matter what you look like, smell like, sound like, or how much money you have.

Hard to grasp, isn't it? Especially in a world that values a certain kind of beauty, a certain type of look and style, and if you don't have it, you don't fit in.

We, as a people, spend millions of dollars, money we often don't have, to look a certain way. We change our hair, our clothes, and our speech, just to fit in. Even those who strive to look different end up fitting in with others. Consider for example the alternative, emo, or goth movements.

Yeah, it is hard to feel valued when society says we're supposed to look like Barbie and Ken, and we *don't* look like Barbie and Ken. However, no matter whether or not we feel valued, it is true—we *are* valued.

Seriously! We *are valued* infinitely, by the Creator of the universe.

Look back in Israel's history. The Israelites wanted a king like the other nations around them had, even though God had told them to have nothing to do with those nations. They wanted to be like everyone else, so they could "fit in." Even though God used Samuel to warn them of the cost, they demanded a king (1 Samuel 8).

So, onto the stage of time steps Saul. He is described like Mr. Universe. He is taller and more handsome than any others in the land. Just what the *people* ordered.

Now, understand me here. God had Saul anointed as king, but it wasn't what He wanted for His people. His desire was that His people would find Him sufficient to fill every need. He knew they wouldn't, yet He allowed this to happen. Sounds backwards, but that's Him in His sovereignty.

Oh, Saul was a handsome devil and was admired by the people. However, after his initial timidity seen in 1 Samuel 10:22, he reveled in his physical attributes. He ate the finest foods, drank the best wines, and threw the best parties, had some incredible victories at war…*and* blatantly disobeyed God by acting as a priest in the tabernacle.

After Saul's one act of utter disregard for God, God removed His Spirit from Saul, and He sent Samuel to Bethlehem to anoint the next king.

In 1 Samuel 16, we find the prophet going to the home of Jesse as God directed, looking for the king that God had chosen to succeed Saul.

Picture it. Visualize it. Samuel walks in, greets Jesse and the missus, and spies the eldest son—a strong, handsome fellow. You know Sam thinks, "How like God to choose a strong leader."

But God speaks to Samuel, saying, "Nope, not this one." And He says that concerning each of the strapping sons of Jesse standing there. Can you just imagine the look of confusion on Samuel's face as he asks Jesse if this is all the boys? Then that look of abject relief when he's introduced to the youngest son, David—even though the aroma of sheep accompanies him—and he hears God's voice telling him this is the one.

Though Samuel lived close to God and had heard God's voice since childhood, he needed the gentle rebuke from the Father, reminding him that *His* measure of a man is not visible to human eyes. *He* looks at the heart.

As believers, we should do the same—look at people's hearts more than their physical attributes. How do we look past the outside to see the inside?

God-goggles.[3]

There's a country song that talks about beer-goggles and the effect that beer has on how a man views life and the people around him, including himself. In the song, this man views himself as very desirable and highly accomplished in all that he tries.

God-goggles are the same. It is the effect that living in a relationship with God has on how we view life and the people around us, including ourselves.

---

3   God-goggles is a term that Darren Wigington, lead pastor of Church of the Cove in Townsend, coined.

With God-goggles, we see all people as loved by God. We can go to third-world countries and see dirty bare feet and unkempt clothes as beautiful. We can see unwashed faces and bodies as precious. The thing is, we have to keep these goggles on at home, too.

You know that kid who came to your church service last week with the spiky hair, low-cut jeans, piercings, and tattoos? Yeah, that one. He's searching for someone, anyone, to love and accept him. He's been told that God will, but it seems like all of God's people just sneer at him.

And did you see that woman with all those kids, all of them clothed in tatters, all smelly and dirty? She's on her own, barely making ends meet, but she loves God with all her heart and wants her children to grow up knowing Him and the love of His people.

Then there's that family that's kind of raucous and rowdy, always interrupting conversations, not the most pleasant to be around, with annoying and undisciplined children. You are picturing them right now, aren't you? That's them. They love the Lord. They dive in to serving Him and to serving others, in any way they can. Sometimes their methods are annoying, but their hearts are pure.

God-goggles help us see the reality in each person we come across, whether at church or elsewhere. Another amazing thing about those goggles is how they help us see ourselves better. Paul said we're not to think more highly of ourselves than we ought, and the God-goggles help with that. Something about spending time in God's presence reminds us of our position and challenges how we relate to others.

Along these same lines, let me share what some would call a radical thought. When it comes to church, sometimes we get the wrong idea. You know what? It doesn't matter to God what you wear to church. He's not even looking at that. He's looking at your heart. He isn't checking out the brand of your jeans or if you are wearing khakis or a suit. He is interested in that which lies within you, and when He sees a heart that longs to know Him, He smiles.

Maybe you are one of those people who has been told you will never amount to anything. Maybe you feel that you never do anything right. You are always messing up. Or you think you are ugly. Maybe you are fat. You are skinny. You are too short. You are too tall. Your hair is the wrong color, the wrong style, or you don't have hair. You are too old. You are too young.

So what?

That's right, so what?

So you don't fit the cookie-cutter pattern that someone else has deemed to be "right." Just how many King Davids did God have in the Bible? How many Solomons? Pauls?

Get my drift?

God loves *you*. He is the One Who created you.

The "you" that you are.

Don't miss that.

The God of the Universe is absolutely *crazy* about you!

That's right. The One who spoke everything into existence is crazy in love with *you*.

Yep, you, right there, the one with this book in your hands. That's right, Y-O-U.

He made you with that crooked little smile that lights up when you see a roly-poly puppy or that special someone. He gave you that quirky sense of humor that shows up at what seems to be the most inappropriate times. He made you with the passions and dreams that you have. Do not dread them! Better yet, *reveal* them! Only then can God use this wonderfully made, incredible creature for His glory and His purpose!

Yeah, that's you again. You are His handiwork. The apple of His eye. The one He died for. The one He's crazy in love with.

Now, whatcha gonna do with that?

Up? Down? Run Around?

...a wrong way to worship?

Lord, I see people arguing over how a person or a church should worship You. Who is right? Which way is right? Is there a wrong way?

What is worship? Is it the time of a church service that includes the music? Is it restricted to a church service? How can we define worship? How do we determine what the right way to worship is? I think first we need to examine some scripture to see what is said there about the topic.

In Genesis 12:8, Abram builds an altar and worships God after hearing a promise from God.

Genesis 26:25 finds Isaac building an altar and worshipping God in response to hearing his father's promised gift confirmed by God.

In Matthew 2:2, we meet the wise men who had been studying for years about the coming Messiah, seeking Him out so they can worship Him.

Matthew 15:25, John 4:24, and Luke 23:47 show examples of Gentiles recognizing and worshipping Jesus.

In Matthew 28:9, Jesus' disciples recognize their risen Lord and worship Him.

Okay, that's nice. What have we learned from this?

First of all, Abram. God called him, and he answered that call with obedience and received a promise of enormous proportions. Hearing all that God had planned for him, Abram chose to gather some stones, build an altar, and worship. I think it is wise to note here that "worship" involved the killing of an animal, including getting the blood all over him and having to clean it up—it wasn't as simple as bowing his head or raising his hands, singing a song, and listening to a sermon. Recognizing himself compared to God required something radical in the way of worship.

Later, Isaac stands in the place of that promise and hears God speak confirmation of that promise into his heart. His response was that of his father; he built an altar and worshipped God.

Both men encountered the God of creation and responded by worshipping Him. Their act was one of choice, involving planning, preparation, work, and then worship. Trouble is we're not told exactly what that looked like. We know that they were familiar with offering a sacrifice on an altar, though, so it is probably a fair assumption that was their act.

Those wise men. How many were there? Be careful! Tradition and songs lead us to say three, but scripture does not tell us. Their gifts were mentioned, gold, frankincense, and myrrh, but not the number of men.

Deeper study reveals that these men were likely the learned advisors and counselors at the royal courts in lands east of Israel—those could be in places we consider Iraq, India, or even China. They could be likened to our Secretary of State and ambassadors to foreign countries, staying up-to-date with their neighboring cultures. These men had probably studied the Jewish writings as well as many others. They had probably studied the skies enough to readily notice that new and different star that suggested to them that Israel was to have a new king.

Those studies led these men to leave home and family and face trials and dangers on the road, just so they could worship Jesus. Their actions show us that there is a right One to worship and that we can and should do whatever it takes to follow Him and get into His presence to worship Him.

Romans, Samaritans, and unidentified Gentiles saw Him and determined Him worthy of worship. At that time, for a Roman to worship anyone other than a Caesar was a crime punishable by death. For a Samaritan, who was actually descended from the Jews, to worship a "Jew" was to betray their family and culture. Yet, they chose to. They recognized God and worshipped Him.

There is no better example of this than the women rushing to tell the disciples of Jesus' resurrection. On their way, they are greeted by Jesus, who they recognize.

Their reaction?

Did they run on to tell the disciples about the empty tomb? Nope.

They ran to Him, grasped His feet, and worshipped Him!

Do you see the recurring theme here?

Recognition.

Abram, Isaac, the Wise Guys, the Roman, the Samaritan, the women—they recognized God, not His physical features. They recognized His majesty, His power, His perfection, His awesomeness. And their reaction was to worship.

David was known as the man after God's own heart. He worshipped. He recognized God and worshipped in many different ways. I, for one, am very glad that one of those ways was to write songs and poetry and that they are preserved in the Bible for us to use today.

I believe worship comes from more than just recognizing who God is. It is only when we also recognize ourselves in relation to

Him that our hearts falter, our minds overflow, we become focused, and thus we worship.

So, the title of this chapter is "Wrong Way to Worship." What's that? So glad you asked!

Depending on who you ask, any or all of the following can be "wrong:"

Raising your hands, not raising your hands

Crying, laughing

Standing, sitting

Kneeling, lying prostrate

Using drums, not using drums

Using instruments, not using instruments

Dancing, not dancing

Singing, and many more…

Yet, as I examine the scripture, I see examples of all of those as acts of worship. Go ahead, look them up, it is a great Bible study.

As we read, we see that we are told to not look at how other religions (nations) worship—to never even think we might want to follow those as an example.

Now, I won't debate all the religions in the world today and the ways they choose to worship their gods, but suffice to say, our best choice will always be to use the Bible as our source for the ways to worship that will please Jehovah, El Shaddai, YHWH, God.

I do, however, want to address one very specific wrong way to worship. It is found in the book of Matthew. Chapter 5, verses 23–24 say, "So, if you are presenting a sacrifice at the altar in the Temple and you suddenly remember that someone has something against you, leave your sacrifice there at the altar. Go and be reconciled to that person. Then come and offer your sacrifice to God."

Now, I'm no theologian, but I think that's pretty plain. Think about what that meant back then. When a person went to the temple, they didn't just go and drop a coin in the offering plate. Their offering was much more. It involved a sacrifice. It involved shedding of blood, some of it getting on the person making the sacrifice.

Can you see that? You've gone to Temple, you've gotten the lamb or doves needed for your sacrifice, you've killed the animal, and now as you stand at the altar, prepared to perform this act of worship to God, you remember that cousin or storekeeper—someone who is mad as a hornet at you. You are covered in blood and about ready to get this over with and get home to clean up and get on with your day. But according to God, you can't. Not yet. You can't even place that animal on the altar fire. Not yet.

You have to leave—which might mean making arrangements with the priest to take care of your sacrifice until you get back—and go talk to that person, make the apology, get the hug, get— and sometimes grant—forgiveness. Restore the relationship the best that you can. Now you are able to come back and place that animal on the fire, performing that act of worship with a clear heart, you know that you and that person are back on good terms and that God sees your worship as right and wonderful.

Still need a modern-day application?

Let me see what I can do.

Imagine it's Sunday morning, right about the middle of the second song. You are singing joyfully, but the memory of that argument you had with your friend last week crosses your mind, including the words at parting, the look on that person's face and the slamming door. You know this friend is still quite angry with you.

According to these words of Jesus, we are supposed to stop our singing, leave our offering in our pocket and slip out of the service, and go directly to that friend to apologize and make every effort at reconciliation with them. Then we can go back, lift our voices in praise, place our tithes and offerings at the altar, and know that God will receive it as worship.

Now I know some of you are thinking:

"What if he won't reconcile?"

"What if I can't find them?"

"What about my rights? I *was* right, you know!"

I think it is safe to say that God is looking for our heart reaction as well as our physical action. He expects us to go and be reconciled if at all possible. He also knows if those people aren't available and whether or not they will forgive and reconcile. However, I believe He fully expects us to do what this verse says.

I think our capacity to worship is diminished by anything that stands between us and God. Sin distorts our view of God, others, and ourselves. If worship is a result of our recognition of ourselves in relation to our holy God, and our ability to recognize God as He is has become distorted, how can we see anything? True worship becomes stunted if not impossible, and anything we do as a rote action that we call worship is just a shadow of the real thing.

A sham. A pretense. A charade.

And it seems that the only one who doesn't see that charade is *us*.

By the same token, our worship is diminished by problems in our relationships. He expects us to try to make peace with all:

"Work at living in peace with everyone, and work at living a holy life, for those who are not holy will not see the Lord" (Hebrews 12:14).

He expects us to live in harmony and unity with fellow believers, saying that the world (lost people) around us will see that and know God's love. Then that means they will come to know God and hopefully worship Him. It's a vicious cycle when we let pride stand in the way of reconciliation. What a victorious circle is completed, though, when we leave that offering at the altar and go.

Are you ready?

HEARTBEAT OF GOD

...pleasing God.

Father, so many people think that rules and checklists are
what please You. I used to think that. They think that a certain
amount of time spent every day reading the Bible and praying is
one more item on their list of things to make You happy. Is that
it? Does checking items off my to-do list please you?

People have sought, for various reasons for many years, to
know the ways to please God. Why that is, I can't say, because from
the earliest times, He's made it quite clear just exactly what that is
that will please Him.

Deuteronomy 10:12–13 explains very simply that God requires
us to reverently fear Him, walk in all His ways, and serve Him with
our entire being.

Well, that's easy enough. This chapter's done.

Oh, you don't think it's that easy? Frankly, neither do I. It takes
quite a bit of work to know what His ways are. It takes time. It takes

a relationship. It takes walking so closely with Him that you feel His heartbeat.

That's not easy, is it? Nope. It means that you will have to do something that is beyond your human capacity. You will have to stop thinking of yourself first—you will have to put God first.

In Micah 6:8, God tells us again what pure faith, or pure religion, is: Do what is right, love mercy, and walk humbly with God. Did you hear it? That's His heartbeat. He wants to see if… no, He requires us to do what is right, to show mercy, and to walk humbly with Him.

Well, doing what's right would seem simple enough, but in the culture we live in, what's right? We live in a world where what our grandparents considered right is now called quaint, antiquated, out-of-touch, prejudiced, and even wrong. We even hear that it is wrong to expect correct behavior, because no one can state objectively what correct behavior is and why.

Almost twenty years ago, I was faced with a teacher who told me that she could not tell the students that something they did was "wrong." She could tell them that their behavior was *against the rules,* but there was no "wrong."

In this kind of environment where there is supposedly no "wrong," how do we do what's right? How do we even know what's right? Simple answer: Measure it by God's yardstick. Know your Bible well enough that when a situation presents itself (and it will), you will know His thoughts on the matter. That's the being so close to Him that you feel His heartbeat.

Let's break this stuff down a little.

Mercy is defined as a blessing that is an act of divine favor or compassion, withholding the punishment or judgment our sins deserve.

Whew! Doesn't it feel great to receive that mercy?

Bask in it. Revel in it.

Oh, and don't forget, we are expected *by God* to show it to others.

That doesn't mean saying, "Bless their heart," after you talk badly about them. That means looking at someone's situation with those "God-goggles" we talked about earlier. See them the way He does. Love them the way He does. Respond to their words and actions the way He does.

That lowlife Samaritan fellow—that's the way the Jews saw him—didn't walk past the man who had been beaten, stripped, and robbed like the church folk did (the priest and the Levite). He stopped his life for a bit and got down in the ditch with the injured man. He covered him up, preserving his dignity; he bound up his wounds, preserving his life. He got him out of the ditch and put him on his own beast, took him to the local Comfort Inn, and cared for him through the night. Then he got his things together the next day, talked to the desk clerk, made arrangements for the man to stay and be taken care of for a few days, then he went on to see to his own everyday business.

There is so much to be learned from this story! Where to begin? First, let's look at the story and liken it to our time.

Mr. Smith, while headed to Atlanta on business, was carjacked. The robbers beat him, took all his money, his car, and even his suit, leaving him for dead on the side of the interstate.

Pastor Dogood was driving along shortly afterward and saw the man lying there on the edge of the road. On a mission to visit with some of his faithful church members, he cautiously slowed down, checked his mirrors, changed lanes, and drove by, certain he would read about the poor sap in the morning paper.

Just a moment or two later, Deacon Handy, known as a godly man down at the local First Something Church, drove down the road, his radio playing worship songs. He spied the lump of hurting humanity lying on the roadside and, like the preacher before him, switched lanes and went on by. Looking back in the rearview mirror, he thought, "That fella should have known better!" Then he returned to singing along with another hymn on the radio.

Then along came Joe. A rough character, Joe was known for being the "wrong" kind of person. He had beer with his meal, he was known to toss some rather colorful language into his conversations, and though he professed to know God, he rarely darkened the door of any church. Seeing the beaten and bloody man in the ditch, he slowed his pickup truck down and stopped. Turning on the hazard lights, he stepped out of the truck, grabbing a blanket he keeps for emergencies.

Stepping down into the ditch, he covered the man's nakedness, taking quick note of his wounds. A barely-breathed prayer of gratitude for the first-aid kit his wife insisted he buy passed his lips as he ran to the truck and reached behind the seat to grab it before returning to kneel at the man's side.

Constantly talking to the man, he used the cleanser from the kit to clean the blood from the man's skin. Then using the ointments, he treated and covered each cut and abrasion. Gently speaking, he helped the man stand and assisted him into the seat of the truck. The thought flickered through his mind that the blood would stain the seat, but the thought was just as quickly dismissed as he reached across the man to fasten the seat belt.

Joe drove carefully to the next exit and pulled into the parking lot of a nice hotel there, securing a room for him and his passenger.

(Side note: Yeah, he might have taken him to a hospital now or just called an ambulance, which, of course, one should do these days, but we're following the story line. Work with me here.)

After settling the man into a bed, he called a local eatery for a delivered meal, which he fed to his patient. The night grew long as he slept fitfully, constantly listening to the breathing sounds in the other bed like a first-time mother listens to her newborn.

As dawn arrived, his patient breathed easier and Joe's pressing need to reach his destination forced a decision. He quietly slipped out the door to visit the front desk. Joe explained the situation to the desk clerk, leaving his credit card on record. He handed the man some cash with instructions to check on the patient, see that he was fed, and to do what was necessary to take care of him. He said, "When I come back through day after tomorrow, I'll settle up with you."

After making a final check on the man and leaving a note with his cell phone number, Joe climbed back into his truck and drove off to his original destination, listening to his favorite country radio station.

Jesus followed the telling of this story with a question—which one was a neighbor? He was essentially asking, which one made God smile? The young man whose heartfelt question prompted this story simply stated, "The one who showed mercy." It wasn't the so-called godly men who didn't even show a thought of stopping their life for this stranger. Instead, it was a man considered by the Jews to not even know God.

So, what do you do in these situations? When you see a homeless person on the street, do you think, "They just need to clean up and get a job," or do you see someone you can help?

Suppose you see a pregnant teenager. Do you tell your spouse that her parents should have taught her better, or do you work with her to see that she and her baby are cared for and loved?

What about the harried waitress at the busy restaurant? Do you tap your foot and drum your fingers on the table? Do you demand further service? Do you think she just doesn't even deserve a tip? Or do you see a woman who needs a word of encouragement?

Could it be that these people made choices that may have placed them in these situations?

Possibly.

Do they need love and hope?

Definitely.

I know, it is tough, but here's where you must decide who matters more, you or the other person?

Ouch!

"But wait just a cotton-pickin' second!" you say indignantly. "I just want to know, what about *my* rights? What about *my* needs?"

Here's a truly revolutionary news flash: You don't have rights. Before you decide to argue the point, read 1 Corinthians 6:19–20. If you are a follower of Christ, you are not even your own.

Let me tell you something, though. There's an awesome thing that happens for you when you do this kind of thing, loving like the Samaritan. Seriously!

Try this experiment: The next time you are in a store or any place where there are weary and frustrated people beside you, walk along and look each one in the face, and if their eyes meet yours, smile. That's it. Nothing major. Just smile.

Now, you will want to watch as you walk by, because you will see many different reactions. You will see looks of confusion that seem to ask if that smile was really for them. You will see eyes roll as though transmitting to you something about the chaos you are both in (or that they think you're nuts for smiling—I'm not completely positive on that one).

Mostly, you will see a change. Nothing earth-shattering or seemingly monumental but what you have just done is make that person feel valued (by looking in their face, in their eyes), and you've shown them hope through your smile. And that, my friend, makes *your* heart lighter. Feel that? It is God's heartbeat.

That's one of the amazing paradoxes of the Kingdom of God. The more we give of ourselves, the more we receive. Go figure!

God designed us to be interactive, and that doesn't mean with a television, computer, iPod, Blackberry, telephone, or robot. It means that we all are searching for acceptance and love. We all like attention, no matter how much or how loudly we decry it. Every person in the world needs acceptance and love, and as believers, we are called to share those things with everyone we come in contact.

However, there's a horrendous risk involved here of which we have to be aware. As with anything in our life, we can let the concept, or the practice, of showing mercy become a mindless, rote action, something we do without thinking or feeling.

Please don't. That makes it fake. The world around us is well acquainted with fakes. We must never join them. We serve a real God, a loving and tender God, a merciful God, and it is our job as His children to portray that—all the time.

Anyone who truly feels God's heartbeat has one major flaw. Their heart and their brain are wired to see needs and help meet them. The concept that they themselves need help is a foreign one and one they must fight.

If you are one of those people who just can't ask others for help, you need to confess that to God and repent. Why is that? Because there is always something that we can't do, something that comes along with which we need help. God designed us that way. He gave each person different talents. He gives believers gifts through the Presence of the Holy Spirit. Paul spoke of those gifts in several of his letters to the churches, explaining that we are designed, *by God*, to fill certain roles within the church—just like different body parts have various roles in our physical body. For instance, you wouldn't expect your foot to see for you, would you? Yet it knows where to step. Why? Because it allows the eyes to help.

There is a lesson hidden in those words. When you refuse to seek help or accept help when it is offered, you deny someone else the opportunity to be a blessing or to use the talents and gifts that God gave them. Shame on you!

God desires for us to live in community. Now, there's a word that's being used a lot these days. What's it mean, really? The Merriam-Webster website, m-w.com, gives this definition:

———————————

1: a unified body of individuals: as **a:** state, commonwealth **b:** the people with common interests living in a particular area; *broadly* : the area itself <the problems of a large *community*> **c:** an interacting population of various kinds of individuals (as species) in a common location **d:** a group of people with a common characteristic or interest living together within a larger society <a *community* of retired persons> **e:** a group linked by a common policy **f:** a body of persons or nations having a common history or common social, economic, and political interests <the international *community*> **g:** a body of persons of common and especially professional interests scattered through a larger society <the academic *community*>

2: society at large

3: a: joint ownership or participation <*community* of goods> **b:** common character: likeness <*community* of interests> **c:** social activity: fellowship **d:** a social state or condition

---

Well, that says a lot. But where does it say anything about God-stuff? It may not mention God directly, but look at what it does say. Community is "a unified body of individuals." Ephesians 4 talks about living in unity complete with instructions on how to do it. And then what does Acts 2:44–47 say? The early believers met together, sharing everything they had, going to the temple together, and having meals together—sounds like community. Unity. Do you see that *"everything* they had" part? Do you think that maybe those who had needs shared those as part of that *everything*? Just something to think about…

So, it seems that God likes community—relationship. Look back in Genesis. He created us—mankind—for relationship. *He* wanted relationship with us. Think about that for a moment.

Let that soak in.

God, the Creator of all that is, *wants* to have a relationship with *you*.

Okay, you can wipe the tears, close your mouth, and begin to read again.

It's an incredible thing to think about, isn't it? God also knew that people need people. He knew that we would operate and survive best in community. He knew that we would need someone with skin on that would look at us and remind us of who we are because of Who loves us. If we will just realize that, too, we'll be much better off. We'll realize that it takes community to help us grow, not only physically but emotionally and spiritually. Having friends in community with us helps us keep our integrity and encourages us in our walk with Christ.

Recently, as I prepared for a group discussion, the thought occurred to me that God expects us to live and believe beyond the life we're living. Not geographically, though I think He desires that, too. What impressed me was to live and think eternally. To understand that whatever we do or say in the next moment matters eternally.

Let that sink in.

You were made by an eternal God.

You were given an eternal soul.

Everything you do or say matters—eternally.

So, you want to know where *that* notion came from? Here it is: When Isaiah told about a child being born who would be called Wonderful, Counselor, Prince of Peace, Mighty God, and

Everlasting Father, he was living in the midst of the nation of Israel, but the twelve tribes were divided—split, separated, and alienated from God and each other.

Here's the story: Ten of the tribes pulled away after Solomon died and were called Israel (there's so much more but that's a whole 'nother story!). Then because of continued unrepentant sin, they fell into the hands of Assyria, never to be seen as a nation again. The remaining two tribes and a few scattered families from Israel were known as Judah. They were also given into the hands of captors, but later their descendants were permitted to return to their land.

It was to these ancestors, the people of his own time, that Isaiah prophesied, telling them about the coming captivity—*before they were ever captured!* He told them all the horrors they would go through, and then shared with them the hope of the Messiah who would rescue them. It was not uncommon to the people hearing this to understand that this wasn't a matter of tomorrow and next week—it was a matter of generations!

Many Jewish people understand hope differently than we who are not Jews. Even now, at their Passover celebrations, they say, "*L'shana ha'ba-ah b'Yerushalayim,*" or "Next year in Jerusalem." They don't mean that they will buy the tickets, pack up their belongings, and make the trip *next* year. Rather they are optimistically looking forward to the Jewish people one day celebrating Passover in Jerusalem every year, fulfilling the ancient dream of *finally* being a free people in their own land. They have, as a nation, understood that the future is not necessarily tomorrow or even in their lifetime. It is the future.

Wow! And we get bent out of shape when it takes two minutes for a traffic light to change. However, my friend, the concept remains the same; what you say and do every moment of every day has eternal ramifications.

Live eternally.

Jonah Trips

...obedience and consequences.

Lord, I believe You called her to a very special ministry, but she's running. She has even turned her back on friends. Help her, please!

You've heard of Jonah, right? He's the guy that ended up in the belly of a fish. Even people who aren't familiar with a lot of scripture know that story, though many miss the reasons as to why it happened, and even more will not admit that we tend, even now, to take that same kind of trip.

A lot.

You do, too.

Sure, you do. Don't deny it.

Why was Jonah in the belly of that fish? Well, let's look back in time a bit. Jonah lived in a time where the neighboring city was one of total decadence. It was the capital city of Assyria, a country known to be extremely vicious in attack and immoral in living.

Nineveh was a beautiful walled city. It covered about 1,730 acres or about 2.7 square miles. The wall around it was about 7.5 miles long with fifteen gates, each named for an Assyrian god. The wall was about 40–50 feet tall (think about a four-story building) and about 50 feet thick (think about how long or wide your house is). There are stories of chariots being driven on top of the wall, side-by-side, for protection.

The atrocities of the people of Assyria are astounding and sickening. The people of the nation are attributed with saying, "We are like an evil rain that washes its enemies away. We are like a net that tangles the feet of those who fight against us."

They were known to skin the bodies of the enemies they'd killed. They would impale their enemies on tall stakes, leaving them to breathe their last breath while watching the destruction of their homes, cities, and families. Their bodies were often left there, on those stakes, lining the roadside into the defeated city, as a warning against anyone who might consider attempting to disobey the Assyrian kings.

It was to these people that God told Jonah to go and speak the words, "Forty days from now Nineveh will be destroyed!"

Jonah knew about the Assyrians. He had traveled around his little area of the world, he knew what they were like, and he did not like the idea that God wanted to give *them* mercy by giving them the chance to repent.

Now, we can believe that Jonah ran the other way out of fear and prejudice, but I think the case pleads best for anger and frustration. He didn't think the people deserved forgiveness, grace, and mercy. I can't say that I would have disagreed with him.

The thing is, though, God loved the people of Nineveh, as horrid as they were, just as surely as He loves you and me; and He told Jonah to go and proclaim His love to them.

Jonah was a prophet of God, educated in the history of his people. He knew of the many times when people turned from God, but then after receiving word of His judgment, repented, and God relented and withheld His judgment. Deep in his heart, Jonah knew that if the people of Nineveh turned to God, then God would not destroy them. Jonah was likely angered by that. He felt they truly deserved destruction and anything else that God would heap on them. Jonah had judged them guilty and had no plan of redemption for them.

Ever been there? Have you ever had the opinion that some people simply do not deserve the grace that God grants because of the way they behave?

Here's the thing, though. Do you believe that you *deserve* God's forgiveness? Do you believe that what you've done merits God's grace or judgment?

Jonah's sense of justice said these people had denied and mocked his God, so they deserved to die. His righteous indignation had no mercy for the heathens. So, when God wanted them to receive a warning, Jonah went right down to the Joppa Travel Agency and booked passage all the way to Tarshish, which appears to be about as far as he could go in the opposite direction.

Before we go further, let's do a little examination of geography. Nineveh was on the banks of the Tigris River, across from the modern-day city of Mosul in Iraq, very much inland from Joppa (today's Tel Aviv), the port city in Israel where Jonah boarded that ship. The city of Tarshish is very likely on the Iberian Peninsula, where Spain and Portugal are. You know, near the Rock of Gibraltar, at the entrance to the Mediterranean Sea. So, to give you a concrete idea about this, there was *no reason* for Jonah to be on a ship in the Mediterranean Sea at all. He didn't have to begin his trip at the docks. His journey was supposed to be inland. The only major body of water he should have crossed on this journey was the Tigris River. Instead of rocking on waves, he should have been shaking sand out of his shoes.

Do you think God was misled as to Jonah's intentions as he neared the gangplank? I've often wondered just how Jonah, who knew God's power and character, thought that he could run away from the direct command of the Creator. Yet how many times do we do the very same thing? We sense the prompting of the Holy Spirit and because it doesn't fit our timing or it requires us to step out of our normal and comfortable life, we wave Him off, or we run. We may not pack our bags and board a ship sailing for a far off port in the opposite direction, but we do it by shutting down our hearts.

Warning!

Alert! Alert! (Picture Robot from *Lost in Space* here.) "Danger, Will Robinson!" (Those of you who don't understand this reference, try Google or YouTube.)

When you ignore, brush off, pass by, or in any other way disregard what God has told you, that's sin, and it places you outside the will of God and outside His protection. No, He doesn't leave you; He promised He would not.

However, you have chosen to walk away from Him.

Consider those times when you have been growing in the Lord, when you were happy and serving Him, then all of a sudden, something happened, something changed. People who were your friends suddenly did things that offended you, said things that hurt you; every sermon you hear was directed right at you; and before long, you had all you were going to take and you wanted out. You stepped onto that "boat" headed in the opposite direction. Before long, you saw even more things change. Circumstances change. Relationships change.

Mostly, *you* changed.

Why is that? What happened? My suggestion is that you go back to your time of growth and examine it. Seek again what God said to you during that time. Personally, I don't think you will have to dig very deep. I think the answer has been ringing in your ears the whole time. Maybe, though, God's call to holiness was more than you could handle, or maybe God revealed an area you weren't ready to give up or deal with, so you bailed. Maybe you felt walls you have had firmly in place breaking down—those walls you've been happily comfortable with—and that has left you feeling more vulnerable than you want. Or maybe His call for you to extend or share His grace just seemed unfair to you.

When the circumstances changed for Jonah, it affected everyone. The great storm was terrifying to the point that seasoned sailors were afraid and casting lots to find out who had brought on this calamity.

When the terrified sailors, who were quite used to the typical Mediterranean storms, woke Jonah—yeah, the paying passenger snoring away down in his comfy stateroom—they quickly learned that he knew exactly what the problem was.

Time out.

Let's stop again for a moment. Jonah messed up, there's no doubt, but when faced with his consequences and how they were affecting others, he knew exactly how to remedy the problem.

There's a mark of maturity there. When we sin, mess up, screw up, or whatever you want to call it, and then recognize what we've done and repent and turn from it, that puts us one step closer to the completeness God desires for us. We are one rung higher on the ladder of maturity when the time between sin, recognition, and repentance grows shorter and shorter. Of course, we would hope that it would get to the place where there is no need at all for repentance, but until the return of Christ, let's strive to recognize sin in our lives quickly and deal with it appropriately.

Okay, back to the ship. Jonah has been awakened and realizes the source of this incredible storm is his disobedience, so he tells the sailors to throw him overboard. I often wonder why he didn't just jump into the water himself. Finally, they listen and reluctantly toss him into the churning waters, where a great fish was waiting for dinner.

Now, can you see this? Scripture says "fish," not whale. Inside it probably wasn't like a huge cavernous room of cartoon fame, and I doubt Jonah found dry firewood and matches. I daresay it was probably dark and smelly with stuff washing around Jonah, bumping against him. Are you saying "Ewww!" yet?

It was within this environment that Jonah spent three days and nights thinking and taking the time to reconsider his actions. Can you say "stubborn?"

Where has God had to take *you* before you listened to Him? Are you there now?

So, our guy Jonah gets tossed up (scripture says vomited or spewed or spit) on the beach and heads inland to Nineveh to share the message that God gave him. Can you just hear the muttering on his journey across the sand and over the mountains? We are told in Chapter 3 that Nineveh was so large that it took three days to see it all. Off Jonah goes, marching into the city, telling them the message God said to tell, and just like he knew would happen, the people repented, God relented, and to be blunt, Jonah was ticked.

This is an important lesson.

God loves people.

All people.

Jesus died for all.

Everyone.

Even the people who have hurt you.

Even the person you despise.

Even the gossip who made up stories about you.

Even the guy who robbed that store.

Even the rapist.

Even the murderer.

E-V-E-R-Y-O-N-E.

To decide that we don't like someone because of their behavior, where they live, or what their ancestors did, or because we think that forgiveness is not for them, means we are missing God's heart on a grand scale.

Have you taken any Jonah trips? Maybe a better question would be, how many Jonah trips have you taken? Now, I don't mean those times when we've backed off on our reading of scripture or our prayer life. That's when we dry up and get blown around like so much dust.

No. I mean belly-of-the-fish trips. Trips where we've heard the call of God, we've been told where to go and what to do, but we turned and ran the other way.

Fast.

Hard.

Our lives now are no different than Jonah's. God calls us just like He did His prophet. And believe me, we hear Him, no matter how we try to brush it off. And God, being God, knows. He knows how we'll react. He knows where we'll run. And just like He did for Jonah, He has a big fish prepared for us.

The length of time we spend inside that stinking, wet, and horrible place is up to us. Jonah lived there three days and nights. It was only after he confessed and prayed, when God told the fish to spit him up on the beach. I've wondered how long Jonah would have stayed in that fish had he been as stubborn as my sons. He might have been in there a lot longer.

So, what's your big fish? Poverty? Jail? Living in a place you don't like? A job you despise? Don't get me wrong. not everyone living in poverty is on the run from God, nor is everyone who is wealthy living rightly with Him. Not every horrid job is a big fish meant to bring a person back to the beach of obedience—but it could be. Some of those fish can be prosperity, great wealth, and fame—things that seem good. Jonah did start out on a Mediterranean cruise, you know.

Running from God is still running from God, and it is just as ridiculous now as it was then. You might even say it is downright stupid.

The choice that we make to say "no" to God's plan for us does not change God's plan. It does change our route of arriving there. It could change the blessing we could have gotten. We might even miss the blessings altogether. His plan will most definitely be accomplished. The thing is, we might be on the outside looking in when we get there.

A key thing to mention here is that God forgives, and no matter if you are on your first Jonah trip or your fiftieth, He's just waiting for you to turn to Him. Read this portion of Jonah's prayer:

While I was fainting away, I remembered the Lord; and my prayer came to Thee, unto Thy holy Temple. Those who regard vain idols forsake their faithfulness, but I will sacrifice to Thee with the voice of thanksgiving. That which I have vowed, I will pay. Salvation is from the LORD.

Not exactly the prayer of a man fully excited to be relinquishing control of his itinerary, but he knew what was required—and he did it.

Sometimes we realize what we need to do, but we're just not "feeling" it. Okay. God knows that. Remember? He goes beyond reading your face like your mother or your spouse does. He reads your heart.

So what do you do? You do what you know is the right thing to do. You praise God—He is God, after all. Then confess your stubbornness—that's just agreeing with Him about it. He knows! He gave you that, but He intends for it to be used *for* Him, not in defiance of Him.

After you've confessed, you have to repent. You have to get off that boat headed the wrong way. You have to turn around, go where He said, and do what He wants. And here's the clincher—tear up the ticket. Don't even go to that travel agent again. There's nothing that God asks you to do that is worse than being in the belly of that fish.

Carefully consider your decisions. Are you going God's way, or are you buying a ticket for a Jonah trip?

FINDING FRUIT

...patience, self-control, kindness, and others.

God! You said I have patience, but I keep losing my temper, and there's little patience in my heart for anyone. I asked You for patience...

"Oh, God, give me patience!" the mother of teens cries out, seeking help from the Lord. Might I suggest that God is looking down at His child saying, "I have, child. Use it!"

When we receive Christ, accept His atoning sacrifice for our sins, and proclaim Him Savior and Lord of our lives, He gives us yet another gift! He gives us the Holy Spirit.

First Thessalonians 4:8b says that it is God who gives us the Holy Spirit. Jesus spoke about One who would come after Him. Paul, in Ephesians 1, said, "And when you believed in Christ, He identified you as His own by giving you the Holy Spirit, whom He promised long ago."

In Galatians, Paul tells us that the Holy Spirit produces fruit in our lives: love, joy, peace, patience, kindness, goodness, gentleness, faithfulness, and self-control. Did you see that? When we invite Christ into our hearts and allow Him to be the Lord of our life, we receive the Holy Spirit who produces fruit in us. And one of those fruits is *patience.*

Sorry to have to tell you, though, it's not automatic, because we are those headstrong, freedom-of-choice-wielding beings that God created. We have a tendency—even though we've accepted Christ—to take the reins back and direct ourselves, getting ourselves into all manner of trouble.

The thing is, when we relax and give all of our will over to Him, He makes some changes. He pulls here, pushes there, tweaks and turns us, and produces feelings and actions that sometimes surprise even us. That's one way we know it is the Holy Spirit.

When we ask God to give us the things that He has already started to produce in us, I believe He answers. However, I believe He answers by providing more opportunities to exercise those new family traits in our life and more ways to flex those new muscles.

Think about the last time you prayed for patience. Oh, go on, you know you have, even if it was barely breathed. Did it seem like the words had barely formed in your mind before you had a screaming child, a demanding spouse, a meddling parent to deal with? Yep, God answered. He didn't give you what you already had; He gave you chances to see it work, chances to use it.

It's in you—it is. So look for it. Use it. Consider some answers to situations that normally throw you out of whack then be prepared to use those solutions. But don't ask for patience. Instead, ask God to show you vividly the places He uses patience and how you can do it, too.

If we were to grasp this concept, what a difference would it make in the house we live—and eventually the world.

GOD LAUGHS

...humor and sarcasm.

Oh! Lord! That's funny! Did you mean for me to laugh there
or am I just weird? Is it really okay if I laugh at stories in Your
Word?

Did you know that God has an incredible sense of humor?
Sure He does! Didn't He create us in His image? That doesn't mean
hair and eyes, folks, that means character, and some of us have
awesome funny bones. That means God has emotions. He laughs.
I personally think He giggled when He made the duck-billed
platypus, perhaps thinking, "There! Let them figure that one out!"

God's very witty. He knows people and our traditions and our
phrases. How many times in scripture did He have a prophet deliver
news with a tongue-in-cheek reference to their silly manmade rules
and traditions?

He (Jesus) used some of those manmade rules and traditions
to teach great truths—usually at the expense of the scribes and
Pharisees, but His mocking of their man-imposed bonds showed
them reality, even if they chose to turn from it.

Humor is an excellent tool to teach truths, yet we, as Christians, tend to shy from it, choosing to be somber in spirit and face. Why is that? Do we see ourselves as more holy if we're not laughing out loud? Do we think that Jesus never enjoyed a belly-laugh? Perhaps we have some sense that laughter will make us seem like the world.

Here's the thing, though, the world around us is stressed to the max. Examples are seen every day:

- Tailgating—I don't mean the football parties, I mean that pushing, shoving, aggravated, stressed-out, spiteful driving maneuver that could be alleviated if we'd just leave fifteen minutes earlier (Egad, did I really say that?).

- Road rage—A term defining that step of stressed-out anger that goes beyond the shouts within one's car to forcing someone off the road and proceeding to tell them in no uncertain terms what they did wrong and how it has ruined your life. Unfortunately, in some cases, this has moved beyond showing someone the middle finger to using a finger to pull a trigger.

- Fights over the most popular gift/toy—Media tells us each year *the* gift to have, and like good little sheep, we follow that. People will slap, shove, push, connive, bribe, lie, steal, or even kill to get *that* gift. Some will go into debt to get something they can't afford.

- People in depression because they can't have what they want.

- Assaults and robberies to get the things they want, the brand they just have to have.

- And the list goes on…

What the world needs to see in those times are genuine smiles and to hear real laughter, not the raucous, worldly laughter rising from jokes made at someone's expense or glorifying immoral behavior.

Remember that verse about being ready to give an answer for the hope inside you? (1 Peter 3:15.) My thought is why would anyone ask you about a hope if it is hidden behind a somber mask of religious piety?

One of the most enjoyable and fun evenings I've ever spent was when a group of Christian friends got together for dinner at a Japanese steakhouse followed by dessert at a franchise-type restaurant with great desserts. We didn't have a problem seating eleven people around the hibachi at the steakhouse but ran into a different situation at the other place.

Being the close-knit group that we were, we asked to be seated at one of the large booths—those are made for six, three on each side. We scrunched up and fit four on each side, two on one chair pulled up to the end, and one on another chair. I have never laughed as hard as I did that night. The people around us heard discussion, laughter, sharing, and "God-talk." They didn't hear dirty jokes or see adult beverages"* delivered to the table. It was fairly obvious to the other patrons that this group of people was "church folks," but they didn't see long faces. They saw eleven people thoroughly enjoying themselves *while* they talked about God!

And then you have to know there are some truly funny things in the Bible, too. Just a few examples—and mind you, this is not meant ever to be irreverent to or about our Heavenly Father. I believe He's the one who pointed these things out to me with a nudge and a chuckle.

First of all, think of Adam. He knows this God pretty intimately, knows He's everywhere and all-knowing, all-powerful, but yet. he tried to *hide*. How silly is that?

And look at Eli's death. First Samuel 4:18 says he fell backward off his seat by the city gate and broke his neck and died because he was old and fat.

Did I just hear someone say "Humpty Dumpty?"

Yeah, I saw that smile.

There is a very serious side to this story, a very sad part, but look how even God used a bit of comic relief in the midst of His story about the capture of the Ark of the Covenant. He could have simply

---

*   While I do not find in scripture that enjoying an adult beverage is wrong, I point this out here to state that the people around us could see our laughter was not because of drunkenness, which *is* denounced in Ephesians 5:18.

said, Eli died, leaving off the old and fat part—but He didn't, and I, for one, laughed.

Take a peek at 2 Kings 2:23–24. It seems that some forty-two or more boys—most versions say youth, so I'm presuming these young men were between twelve and thirty (since this is talking about Jewish culture)—come out and mock the newly anointed prophet, Elisha, calling him names, in particular "Baldy" (or something similar). So, here this man stops his journey down the road, turns and looks at these boys, and curses them in the name of the LORD. (I don't believe that involved what *we* call curse words.)

Right then, with no hesitation, two bears (some versions define them as she-bears) come out of the woods and maul them. That is, those Mama-Bears tore those hateful boys up.

Now, in my admittedly strange sense of humor and Southern upbringing, I see a picture here that causes me to put my hand over my mouth and laugh out loud. I know if someone were to see me, they'd wonder what brought on the merriment. How I would explain that, I'm not quite sure.

Once again, it is a very serious situation. Elisha has just seen Elijah taken up to God in a whirlwind—and that's a story unto itself—but here's this man who has just seen God's power, and he's trying to get on to his next destination, when these fellows come out mocking him. My mind has conceived several "movies" of this incident. Go with me here.

Scene Version I: It's a hot and dusty road that Elisha is walking on from Jericho to Bethel. Suddenly, this large gang of tough-mouthed young men steps out, circling around him. (Think *West Side Story*.) See the leather, hear the chains! Mocking and taunting him, never fearing any consequence, the gang even (in my imagination) pushes him back and forth between them. Finally Elisha looks at the young men and speaks a curse in the name of the LORD. The leader of the gang's eyes flicker with the tiniest glimmer of fear before he snickers at Elisha's attempt to fight back. Then he sees these two bears, only two, tearing up his gang. Two bears unleashing some Chuck Norris moves against forty-two men and boys.

Scene Version II: Elisha's walking along the road, looking from the low place of Jericho, near the Dead Sea, up toward Bethel in the mountains and is suddenly confronted with a bunch of guys ranging in age from youth to manhood. They're mocking him, chanting uncomplimentary things about his baldness. He curses them, invoking the LORD's help. Suddenly, out from the woods step what appears to be two bears, instead are mothers that know these boys all too well. Swinging wooden spoons, belts, and fingernails, these matronly terrors work those boys over, sending them squalling.

Okay, yeah, I know it's a strange sense of humor—I did warn you. But the point is, again, God knows that our human minds and hearts can only take so much heavy understanding, regardless of how tough we try to be. I believe He allows those bits of laughter

to break us out of that reverie of focus and lighten our hearts.
I mean, He put these two verses right there as a tag on chapter two,
before we go on to learn about another king.

Why?

It wouldn't have changed any of the amazing miracles God
did through Elisha in the previous verses had He left them out. So,
why?

Yes, to remind us that mocking God's chosen has
consequences, but I believe He enjoys that look of confusion
that He sees when we come to places like that in His Word.
I think He likes hearing a giggle when one of His children gets a
mental picture. I think He loves us enough that He gave us this
thing called humor and wit, and I believe He loves to hear the
laughter of His children.

If you have children, you understand this. Think about how you
feel when they start with one of those little giggles that grows into
a full-blown belly-laugh. Do you smile? Do you join in the laughter?
God *is* our Father, you know.

Sometimes we just need to remember that we were created
in the image of God. The "likeness," not the "lookness." He gave us
feelings and emotions, and there's nothing at all wrong with any
of those. Just like with anything else, it is what we do with those
emotions that can become a problem.

Our laughter should never be at someone else's expense. We should always show love and compassion, just like our Lord. We must be certain that our mirth and merriment is never detrimental to the cause of Christ.

THIS IS GOOD?

...understanding His thoughts.

*I've been thinking about my past, Lord, 1990 and '91 in
particular. I was so sure You'd fix things to be 'good'—I just
never knew that Your idea of good was so good!*

At age twenty-seven, I was quite suddenly faced with the reality
of a husband who was having an affair. I wish I could tell you that I
dealt with that in godly ways, but I didn't—not at first, not always.
Tears, screams, arguments, and poor choices were my norm until I
remembered something. I knew my Bible said in Romans 8:28 that
all things work together for good, so I started to trust in that. A
loving friend pointed me to Dr. James Dobson's book, *Love Must Be
Tough,* which showed me that I wasn't. Tough, that is.

The premise of the book was that whether it be a spouse or
other family member living in a way that is 1) displeasing to God
and 2) harmful to themselves and/or their family, then the one who
loves them has to be tough enough to make them face a choice.
The choice is to either give up that behavior and/or addiction or
give up their family. It's not easy to get to that place where you
are ready to say that, because the loved one just might choose the

RAMBLINGS FROM THE SHOWER

other person, the addiction, or the behavior over you. You have to be ready for that, and you have to stand tough. In my case, it took several months after reading that book before I was ready to present the choice: The girlfriend goes or your family does. No middle ground. Think intervention.

Getting to that place was a long, hard journey. It was also one that had some potholes along the way, but I continually trusted and spoke aloud my belief in Romans 8:28.

In October of that year, when I gave him the choice and told him not to come home again until he'd made the decision, he spent a couple nights away (spending one with his father who was very old-fashioned and quite vocal about how things should happen). Finally, the decision was made, the girlfriend would be gone. I rejoiced and praised God for making things good.

A scant couple of months later found us celebrating Christmas. His job forced him to be at work that afternoon and evening. Being East Tennessee, where the weather can change twice in an hour, it grew very cold as the day wore on. It changed from a reasonable temperature to a need-your-heavy-coat one. My husband had left his coat at home, so our son and I loaded into the car to drive the hour and a half to take care of Dad, excited that we would be able to visit with him.

This was in the old days, before cell phones were inexpensive and readily available, and besides, we wanted to surprise him. He, however, was not the only one surprised.

Upon arrival at his workplace, I saw her car. The girlfriend was there at his workplace with him.

You know, sometimes, God protects us from ourselves. He did that day by means of my husband's partner, who finally responded to my banging on a not-supposed-to-be-locked door. He wouldn't let me in. I can still see him blocking my way, telling me that I didn't need to go in there as he listened to my ranting about how he'd just better move and let me in.

Yes, God rescued me there, because I was choosing anger and rage as my reaction to seeing that car.

The eventual outcome of that day was my heart wondering, "What happened to the good?"

It wasn't even a full year later, after my husband had changed jobs, that our marriage was again rocked by infidelity, and this time, when given a choice, he chose denial.

Oh, how I cried out to God! At times, I could picture myself beating my fists against His chest as I cried, "Why?" I kept asking where Romans 8:28 was. And you know, He didn't mind. He held me as I cried. He listened to my railings. He heard my fears. He protected me from so many things during that time, even when I stepped away from church—again.

There were people around me who were doing drugs and other things, but to be honest, no one ever offered any to me. I fully believe God had this glowing neon sign on me that told them not to.

Where was the good? I didn't see it as I sat in the attorney's office ironing out the details to file for divorce. I didn't see it as I worked two jobs trying to make ends meet—ends that sometimes never even saw each other. I didn't see the good as I watched my son try to fix his parents, so his world wouldn't fall apart.

What I didn't know then was that God's thoughts are nothing like mine. His ways are higher than mine, His thoughts higher.

I've learned since that time, nearly twenty years ago now, that God was right there, working everything out for good. The thing was, my idea of "good" was different than His.

He gave us all free will to make choices, and boy, do we make some doozies! I had chosen to marry primarily to get away from home. No, don't ask me why I didn't just go to college instead, I can't answer that. (I got an education, though.) In that same will, I chose to not read His Word regularly, not to attend church often—though I did, from time to time, when I could afford the clothes for my son and me. Wait, isn't there something about that in another chapter?

So, my husband at the time made his choices. How incredibly grateful I am that our Heavenly Father was there, waiting on that front porch for His prodigal child, because when I finally turned back toward Him, I didn't have to go far. The chorus of a song recorded by Phillips, Craig, and Dean says:

―――――――――――――――

The only time I ever saw Him run was when He ran to me,

He took me in His arms

Held my head to His chest, said

"My son's come home again"

Lifted my face, wiped the tears from my eyes

With forgiveness in His voice He said,

"Son, do you know I still love you?"

He caught me by surprise when God ran.

―――――――――――――――

I felt that. He lovingly and so tenderly embraced me, welcoming me back to Him, binding my wounds, and forgiving my sins. Now *that* is good!

Yet, I was still very much a broken woman, divorced and so unsure of myself or life in general. The one thing I was sure of was that God had said "good" and I would trust Him for that, even when I couldn't see it.

I am by no means saying that God ordained or advocated my divorce. His Word is very explicit in telling us that He hates it. It was yet another choice that I made. Another sin that I chose and one more that He forgave. Thank You, God.

Well, God's "good" turned out to be a godly man who loves the Lord simply and boldly. A man who understands and displays unconditional love, and his choice was and is to love me, and my son. God's "good" involved two stepsons, in-laws galore, a home that is steady, and best of all, Him. He has drawn me to His side, taught me, and grown me to this place where I can share these bittersweet memories with you.

I can see now that God took the choices I made and worked them all together for good—*His* version of good.

So, you're in a situation where you find that your wrong choices or the choices of others have landed you. You can see it's not good. Your aching heart tells you with every beat that it's not good. So, what do you do? Here's the formula, don't miss it!

Trust Him to keep His Word!

He said that He will use the place that you are in and it all will work out for good. The thing is, you have to get your focus right. You have to see that "good" the way God does. The only way to get your focus right is to draw near to God. In James 4:8, He said that when you do, He'll draw near to you. God promised that when you seek (search for, keep looking for) Him with all your heart, He will be found. Read Jeremiah 29:13 again.

Let me warn you, though. It won't be easy. It is never easy to relinquish control. The training you will gain from this experience is eternal, and you simply cannot miss even one part of one lesson. You will cry, you will laugh, you will feel your lowest and your highest, but I can promise you one thing, that roller coaster ride will make you a different person than the one who started it.

Always trust. God does have a plan for your life and even you can't stop it.

Healing

...God's sovereignty.

I'm not sure I get this, God. She had melanoma, and You
took it away. He died of liver cancer. We asked You to heal
them both.

The year 2000 was a special year in so many ways. Every media
source around was looking at history—all the changes that had
occurred in the newly ending century.

Some wonderful ones include indoor plumbing, electric
appliances, air conditioning, microwave ovens, and cellular phones.
Think about it; imagine your world without those.

Our nation was in the throes of a presidential election. My
husband and I celebrated the ninth year of our honeymoon—okay,
it's mushy, but it has been amazing!

Then, at the end of March, we heard news that we never
expected: "Cancer"—more precisely, malignant stage III melanoma.

Earlier in the month, my hair stylist saw a growth on the upper edge of my left ear and insisted that I have my dermatologist look at it. Good thing I had already made an appointment for the next day, she was ready to whup me! That's a friend, not just a stylist. The next day, the doctor removed that growth and sent it to the lab, sending me home with the soothing words that it didn't appear to be anything at all.

Time out.

At that appointment, while I waited to see the doctor, I read an article on Maureen Reagan, daughter of former U.S. President Ronald Reagan. She had, at that time, struggled with malignant melanoma for several years. The article talked about all the things involved and what the disease had done to her body since it invaded: the constant tiredness, the battle of any illness, because the disease ravages the lymphatic system. It included the risk factors (remember, at this point, I didn't know I had it, I was just reading along), which told me that I had three of the five listed: light skin (can we say pale white?), light eyes (blue), and sunburned repeatedly as a child (only every time I went outside).

Another part of that article talked about the care, surgery, due diligence, mapping, and all kinds of good things to know in case you ever got melanoma. I filed that back into the recesses of my mind, so if someone I ever knew got the diagnosis, I'd be ready to share with them.

What's the amazing miracle here is that I read an issue of a dermatologist's magazine instead of *People* or *TIME*. I believe that God in His sovereignty knew I'd need that information to help soothe me and sustain me, so He gave me the hunger that day for something outside my normal fare.

Now then…The Day. Here's a word for doctors and their staff: *Don't* call someone at work and tell them the doctor needs to "see you immediately" without giving any other information. For Pete's sake! Consider how you would feel getting that kind of phone call! Obviously staff can't share that kind of news on the phone, but something needs to be fixed here.

Anyway, back to the story.

Having heard that this busy doctor had cleared a space for me to come in to talk to him that afternoon, I knew it wouldn't be good news. In tears, I called my husband, then a close friend, and then our pastor. To say I was a basket case that afternoon would be like saying Texas is a wide spot in the road.

I faced the doctor and heard the words; although after hearing the word "cancer," I think my mind went on auto-pilot. The doctor made an appointment for me with a specialist in facial tumors, and I left. My darling husband met me there in the parking lot and bravely prayed with me, telling me we'd conquer this somehow. I was numb and he was reeling.

The news from the specialist wasn't all that great either. As with all cancers, they try to get rid of all the abnormal cells, which means cutting a wide swath around the site of the tumor. Take a look at your ear. Just how much room do you see there?

Because of the size of the tumor was the size that it was, the *least* they would take was the top third of my ear; thus giving me the option to leave it or have reconstructive surgery. The other option was to remove the entire outer ear and set it up for a prosthetic ear. It was at this point that I felt panic, which I'm sure the doctor sensed. He told us to discuss the options, and then come back and give him an answer.

On top of having to make that kind of choice about my ear, he told me they wanted to remove the neck and facial lymph nodes—all of them. That would mean a scar across my face and on my neck down to my shoulder.

My faith is, I suppose, a strange thing. I will believe in God and believe quite simply that He is God, all-powerful, all-knowing, and perfect. People, on the other hand, I don't trust in so completely. I went home and began my research, because I was quite certain that this doctor had not given me all the options.

My research dug up information about a procedure called a sentinel node test. This test consisted of an injection at the point of the tumor with a radioactive isotope. Then using an active CT scan, the radiology doctors would follow that isotope to the first lymph node it traveled to, the sentinel. The theory is this is the same path that the melanoma cells would have followed. Then the doctor would mark that as the first node and send me to surgery. The surgeon would excise the area where the tumor had been, but rather than removing nine or ten lymph nodes, only one would be removed and would be sent straight to the lab. The next step depended on the results from the lab. If there were melanoma cells anywhere in that sample, they would take the next node and do the same testing. This would continue until they reached a cancer-less node, the idea being that you only take what is truly necessary.

Armed with my information, we returned to the surgeon's office to discuss our plan. It was such a blessing to learn from our first question that he is a believer in Christ and trusts Him for all he does. He also shared that he too is a cancer survivor—melanoma, even! Amazing the comfort I found in that revelation, though I can tell you I was somewhat surprised to have a doctor pull his shirt open to show us his scars.

He graciously, with a smile, listened to my questions about the sentinel node test, saying he thought that was an excellent option for me. Then he asked if I had decided on excision or amputation. Oh how we all laughed when I said, "Doc, I barely remember to put earrings in my ears when I leave home, how will I remember to put on an *ear*?"

While this is still the source of laughter, I was actually quite serious. I didn't want to lose more of me than was necessary, so we opted for excision.

Meanwhile, my son had gone into the Air Force the previous summer. Just a side note: San Antonio in August is *miserable*. (Wonderful city but the heat and humidity are excruciating.) He was planning to get married mid-April.

Did you notice the time line? I pitched it rather fast, so here you are again: I was diagnosed at the end of March, and his wedding was two weeks away. Now, I'm no fashion maven, I hadn't even tried on a dress in a couple years, but I didn't relish the idea of a turban hair design for my son's wedding. So I asked the doctor if we could put the surgery off till after the wedding. His reply was that since the tumor itself was gone, any internal damage that was going to be done was done, so if I were willing to wait, he wasn't opposed to it. The surgery then was scheduled for the Tuesday following the Saturday wedding.

So, you saw the heading of this chapter, "Healing" and expected me to tell of a miracle healing. Well, here's my thought: God said He would show favor on whom He chooses.

Exodus 33:19 says, "And He said, 'I Myself will make all My goodness pass before you, and will proclaim the name of the LORD before you; *and I will be gracious to whom I will be gracious, and will show compassion on whom I will show compassion*' " (emphasis mine).

I believe that includes those miracles. Why wouldn't He choose me? I don't know. Isaiah 55:8 says I can't possibly understand:

'My thoughts are nothing like your thoughts,' says the Lord. 'And my ways are far beyond anything you could imagine. For just as the heavens are higher than the earth, so my ways are higher than your ways and my thoughts higher than your thoughts.'

I believe that He knew that my telling of the story would touch lives in ways that a miracle healing wouldn't. Sometimes the miracle is in the journey of faith that we take; and that journey was summed up in a statement to my mother as we drove to pick my son up at the airport for his wedding. I told her the things I'd been feeling. I knew that, as a mother, she was struggling with the possible loss of her child. I wasn't sure how she would take my words, but I had to share.

I explained that I knew that I was healed of all cancer, but I didn't know where I would *see* that, here or in Heaven.

That is my understanding of my miracle. God didn't prompt me to not have the surgery. He led me to go through that with faith knowing that healing was mine—He just didn't say if it would be here on Earth. It wasn't something to take lightly, and I didn't. It is not easy to say to your mother that God just might choose to heal you by taking you to Heaven, but sometimes you have to just trust that God knows better than you what that other person needs to hear.

So, now when I hear someone praying to see their miracle, I wonder if they know what they are asking for. I haven't seen any place in the Word where God promises our instant or full healing in this time of our life on Earth.

Now, there was that time in Numbers 21 where the Israelites whined and spoke against God and had to deal with fiery serpents. In that instance, He used His official spokesman, Moses, to craft a pole with a replica of those serpents on it. When bitten, if a person looked to that pole, he would be healed and live. I don't think that applies to the here and now, mainly because it was in answer to a God-judgment on a specific people at a specific time.

I think that we humans forget sometimes that our life is eternal. Our life continues without end once it starts. Believer or not, we'll live someplace forever.

I believe that when we forget that our life does not end when our time on Earth does, we misunderstand healing. We must realize that God doesn't do things under the constraints of time, space, or our very limited understanding. Our healing may happen when we step across that threshold between the life on Earth and the life in Heaven—all we do at that point is change residences, not lives. Our neighbors, the people whose lives we are actively part of, will be different, but we will be us. Our healing may happen the moment we seek God's face for it. That's up to the Sovereign Lord Who knows all things and how our healing will glorify Him.

This is an important concept to teach our families. We need them to know that life isn't over when we die. We need to live our life every single day, with the realization that we are eternal beings making choices that have eternal ramifications, but also with the recognition that we only have a very few days to make those choices. We can't procrastinate!

Sometimes we think our newfangled ideas and ways are superior to the old-fashioned ones. But we, in our infinite wisdom, or lack thereof, have worked to insulate ourselves and our children from the reality of death.

My first mother-in-law died of non-Hodgkin's histiocytic lymphoma. She and my son had a very special bond that was amazing to watch.

My son and I had moved in to my in-laws' home during her last month of life on Earth, to take care of Granny. He would sit by her on her bed and "read" to her like any loving three-year-old grandson would. When it came time for him to go outside to play, he would pat her hand, kiss her cheek, and tell her he would be back in a little bit.

The morning of her death, I called my mother to come and take my son to her house for the day. My thought was to prevent him pain by not seeing Granny die. We had not revealed to him that she was at death's door, but I can remember, clear as day, when he was ready to leave, he patted her hand, kissed her cheek, and said, "Good-bye, Granny." It was as if he knew without anyone telling him that she would not be there when he returned.

I still tried to protect my son the day of the funeral. A friend took him out for the day, and he had loads of fun, but I took something away from him that I cannot give back. I took away his chance to truly say good-bye to his beloved grandmother. (I'm sorry, son.)

Way back when, before telephones and television and cars and computers made our life so "easy," we spent time with our families. We'd share life with one another. We grew up knowing that death is real but another part of life. It was just as much a part of life as growing up, going to school, getting married, and having children. We understood that it was permanent and that losing someone we love hurts, but we didn't fear it to the point of ignoring it or trying to avoid its very existence.

Another by-product of ignoring the reality and finality of death is a generation (or two) that has no real understanding of their need for salvation.

All that to say this: Don't insulate yourself or your family from the pain and grief of death. It happens. It's real. And we hurt. But we learn that it's not to be feared. We learn the value of life, and if we do it right, we learn that value before it is too late.

James tells us our life is a vapor—gone so quickly. That's our time here—the year or ten or seventy or however many we get. We are promised eternal life *with Him* that starts when we receive His gift of salvation.

That puts a different slant on things, doesn't it? So, where are you on this journey? Have you heard the words "terminal" in regard to your health or that of a loved one? Seek their healing. Approach the throne and seek God in this matter. If He directs you to doctors and surgery, go boldly and know He is in control. Realize, however, that His choice for your journey may be different than what you are seeking.

We have a friend who recently went through a bout with pancreatitis. His treatment seemed to go well, and then he bottomed out—spending several days at death's door. Every doctor, nurse, and lab technician knew of his faith and saw the trust he and his wife have in God. We don't know fully at this time just how that has affected lives, but we know it has. We don't know yet why God chose to spare his life, but He did. Our friend is certain God has plans for him and is seeking to learn those.

Always remember, your healing will happen, not because of the force of your faith, but because of the mercy and grace of our loving God—and in His timing. It may well happen when you speak deliverance from the disease. Then again, it may happen on the other side of this vapor we call life.

STICKS AND STONES

...abusive relationships.

So many people live in fear of their lives, Lord—being abused in various ways. I see it in the news, I hear it on the radio, and I've lived it. Why? What's the deal? Why do people work so hard at manipulating others?

This is by far the hardest chapter I will share with you, and I find myself writing it to at least four audiences: people who are abused, people who abuse others, people who are teetering on the edge of abusive relationships, and people who know and love others in one of those situations.

If you are in an abusive relationship, hear me: You are not alone. There are others who have been where you are and have made it out. But hear me in this, too: You will not change the abuser. You cannot fix this person. That's God's job, but He won't do it against this person's will.

If you are an abusive person, you need to admit it. You need to recognize yourself in the words you are about to read and accept that you are an abuser. I pray that at that point you will do whatever it takes to get help to make the changes that need to be made. Not the temporary ones you've made before—the kind that will last through your lifetime.

If you are questioning if the relationship you are in might be abusive, it quite possibly is. It might be time to step back and examine it in the light of day with some God-help. Ask Him. He'll tell you.

If you breathe, you know people who are in abusive relationships. You may not see the bruises, but soon you'll be able to recognize them. As I said, you can't fix that. You can't jump into that relationship and mend the broken heart or fix the problems. You can love them both. You must. God will hear your prayers; pray them.

Abuse. A major topic of discussion these days. Is it new? I don't think so; I think abusive people have been around since the fall of man. What's abuse borne from? Jealousy? Insecurity? There are many theories and much discussion but no real solutions. Having survived an abusive relationship, I believe I can share with the voice of experience, and I will share about male abusers of women. I know it goes the other way as well. That is just as horrible as what I'm sharing, if not more so. Abused men generally have no outlet, no one who understands their victimization.

What I can tell you, having been there, is that the solutions go unheard by the one being abused and the one doing the abusing. The first is unable to hear because she is protecting herself by watching her words and actions to avoid the wrath of her abuser.

The second is unable to hear because he doesn't see himself as an abuser.

Sadly, the signs of abuse aren't as visible as a large flag waving over someone's head. How I wish they were! In my situation it would have saved a lot of heartache, but then again, I wouldn't be the person I am today, and I wouldn't be able to share this with you. Please, don't get me wrong. My first marriage had some wonderful moments, one of which was the birth of my amazing son. Another was getting to know my in-laws and visiting in the mountains where I now live. There were good times, but there were bad. Those are the things I need to share now.

My own story is one of living with low self-esteem. I knew my parents loved me, yet there was a sense of little worth. Everyday I would come home from school to my mother watching soap operas. She would have me get a snack and head to my room to do my homework. Not a bad thing in itself, but if I wanted to share my day, whether good or bad, I had to wait. Around the dinner table, we'd have the TV on, watching Walter Cronkite report the news. In the mid to late 1960s, this meant I heard a lot about the war in Vietnam and "those damned hippies," who protested the war. Often when I would try to tell about my day, some event that was significant to me, I would be told to hush, with a finger pointed to the TV. It was unspoken, but I knew what was more important to my father at that point.

Just a side note: You know how people say that abuse is generational? That a person who grew up with abuse will become an abuser? Unfortunately, I learned that's true. I realized one day, as I sat watching *General Hospital* when the boys arrived home, I was so absorbed in the "life" on the TV that I was ignoring my children's lives. What a revelation. I shut off the daytime dramas in 1994 and have yet to watch them again. Frankly, I haven't missed them at all.

Back to the story: In school, I was rather disliked, because I tended to be the kid with the answers. You know the one who messes up the grading curve? Yeah, that was me. Sorry. It also didn't help that I was chubby and wore clothes purchased at the five and dime. I felt and heard the condescension of other students. When in fifth grade, my being a "teacher's pet" cost me my wallet being stolen.

In high school, I got myself into trouble trying to be with a guy that I should have just said no to. Running from the shame of that, I convinced my mother to put me in the brand-new Christian school our church was opening. She went to bat for me with Dad, who thought paying for an education I could get for free was ridiculous. He didn't like the church anyway, which made it that much worse. As a result, I worked with the younger students to offset my tuition. It was cool being a "teacher" at fifteen (and I was so qualified, of course!).

I tried to prepare myself for getting out in the world by getting my dream job. When I applied for a job at the Magic Kingdom of Walt Disney World, they didn't like girls "onstage" to look chubby. They informed me that for my height, my weight was too much. I was crushed. Especially when I'd seen girls working in the park who were my size or larger. So, I did what any teen-aged girl would do. I buckled down and lost the weight. I was a solid size eight the next time I applied. When they told me that my weight didn't fit their parameters, I challenged them. A bold step for me, but I took it. They sent me to the wardrobe area where I learned that even though I didn't fit the parameters, I did fit the costumes.

It was with this mindset that a seventeen-year-old, socially inept, and uncertain girl stepped into the world of social life. I desperately wanted a boyfriend. I desperately wanted friends, period. So, when this guy started paying attention to me, I didn't just respond, I drank it in. I gobbled it up. I fell for him, head over heels. Before the summer was over, he took me to the top of the Contemporary Hotel at Disney World and proposed. What a romantic! I quickly agreed to marry him, and only a couple weeks after he turned eighteen, we were wed.

It wasn't long before it started. I've always dealt with my weight. My first diet was at age twelve. I should have gotten a clue when my new husband flatly told me one night, "If you ever get as big as your mother, I'll divorce you." That *should* have been a huge red flag, but I refused to see it wave and instead worried almost constantly about my weight.

Since we married right out of high school, finding work was difficult. I worked at grocery stores and other retail stores while he worked in an Orlando tourist attraction and attended courses at night to become an emergency medical technician. We'd been married less than five months when I found out I was pregnant.

Here I should have seen another red flag waving when my parents and his parents were excited about the baby, but all we did was argue about how we'd support it. I wasn't excited; I was worried. Oh, there were times when I was excited. That butterfly flutter of his first movements inside me were indescribable, but the joys I've seen other mothers have about setting up their baby's room and making preparations for the new life just weren't there. The sense of care and nurture I've seen in other soon-to-be fathers wasn't there. I felt like I'd messed up, that I'd caused us undue stress, and it was my problem to solve.

Unfortunately, one of the biggest problems with my pregnancy was that I put on weight. Admittedly, I gained a lot of weight. I didn't feel pretty anyway, so, really, what difference did it make? I guess it was my way of punishing him for not just loving me. I had seen this kind of behavior from my own parents. It's not pretty; it is what it is.

When my son was a couple years old, in an effort to feel desirable to my husband, I joined him in looking at pornography. I suppose I thought that it would somehow fix things, make us work better together. As I look back from a state of health, I wonder where that insane notion came from, but back then, it made sense.

Later, when his mother died, he went to school to get a degree in paramedic technology, and we moved to Tennessee to live in our dream place. I was so excited. I just knew that getting him to a place he loved would make our lives much more enjoyable and much richer. For a while, it *was* good. Then he was transferred to work in a town about two hours away. I guess there's something about distance from home for a forty-eight-hour period and being in the presence of someone who believes all you tell her that can cause a man's brain to stop thinking logically. What I was told when I learned of the affair was that "she *understands* me." The tough part of this was that it was my fault, or so I was told. If I had been a better housekeeper, better in bed, better cook, better organizer, prettier, more understanding, more anything, he wouldn't have given her a second glance.

As you've learned in another part of this book, which you've stuck with for some strange reason, he gave up that affair. He changed employers, placing him just minutes from home instead of hours. Trouble was, he ended up spending a lot of time with another woman who was thin, pretty, and "understanding," and another affair begun.

All the while, I was told how the people where he worked thought of me as a shrew, a whining wife, a nag, a whore, and so many more things I refuse to recall. I guess that was so that I wouldn't show my face there, thus making it easier to enjoy his time with his co-worker/lover. The abuse I endured was, for the most part, mental and emotional. There was only one time that he actually physically attacked me.

One of the things battered women learn—and I personally think battering includes those years of hearing how stupid and incompetent they are—is how to push buttons. They know what things will sting the most when they say them in the heat of an argument. The trouble is they think that it will just result in more screamed insults, when sometimes it actually provokes a physical attack.

Such was my case. I knew the name I was about to call him would rile him, and I used it. I expected him to once again storm out of the house, by now a regular occurrence, to go and spend another night with *her*. I miscalculated. Instead, when the last syllable passed my lips, I found myself bent backwards over the arm of a chair with his hands around my throat. Kicking and screaming and clawing, I managed to escape that grasp, only to be tackled from behind as I tried to run to my son's room. My son had awakened, grabbed the phone, and walked into the living room to find his father sitting on his mother's back with his hands around her throat, trying to choke her. As he attempted to dial 911, the man who was my husband stood, moved quickly within range, and kicked the phone from my son's hands.

To be perfectly honest with you, the next few moments are a blur in my mind. I think I told him to get out and never come back. I don't know if he realized what he had done and left on his own or what. What I do remember is that the next day I filed for divorce. I don't know if I would have stayed if he had only hurt me, probably so, "for the sake of the child," but since he'd attacked him, too, I wanted out. I wanted to feel safe. I wanted to feel loved.

I confess I sought solace in places I shouldn't have. First, I began working out at a gym with a passion. If you've ever wondered, a woman can lose weight and survive on a Milky Way and Lay's

Potato Chips diet. Just so you know, though, it required working a grueling weight circuit five days a week for three solid months. I looked good—sort of. I was skinny, thinner than I'd ever been. I could bench press more than some men I knew. I bought new clothes—provocative ones. I didn't mind being admired by men. I didn't mind flirting with them. I didn't scorn their advances. It was a poor choice and was also the reason I didn't file for divorce for adultery and instead chose irreconcilable differences. I've since laughed and said that our irreconcilable difference was that he wanted a girlfriend *and* a wife, and I couldn't reconcile to that.

From the studies I've read, most boys and men who are abusive start their relationships in the same way. They are charming and delightful to be around. Then, as the relationship grows, their moods swing. They will talk often about how misunderstood they are in the workplace or at home. They are mistreated. Women are by and large nurturers to some extent. Few of us can stand to see someone hurting or mistreated. That's where we get caught. Our hearts, already tender for this person, melt even more when we think about someone betraying him or causing him angst. So, we bond tightly with him, becoming his champion and guard.

Once the object of the abuser's affection begins seeing things his way, he stakes his claim, ever so cleverly. He will draw her away from anyone who might see through his charade and help her to see it too, whether it is friends or family, thus isolating her with him. He will talk about how that person hates him, or this one lies about him. All things he knows will draw her closer to him and away from them.

The abuser will be so sweet, though. He will have some cute little pet names for her—in public, anyway. In private, the names are more like barbs speaking to her monumental flaws like her being overweight or unable to cook or only a high school graduate—all horrible things he has to deal with. Mine? "My plump little pigeon." It is all part of the anatomy of an abusive relationship. He must break down any sense of self-worth she might have. He must isolate her from anyone who might speak worth and real love into her life. As time goes on, she will believe his words about her. She will be convinced there is no one else on the planet that would or could even put up with her. If it were any other man, she'd already be out on the streets. She becomes very appreciative that he's so benevolent. Besides, he tells her, if she leaves him, he will do himself harm. If she's not by his side, he might as well die. And there's that threat of "If you leave, I'll file for divorce." If version one doesn't keep her there, then one of the others will. Manipulation and mind games are an abuser's main weapon, and he's a ninja at using them.

Those of you who have never lived through this are probably wondering how a woman could allow herself to accept that or how she could allow it to continue. That's a tough one to understand, and I'm not sure I can aptly explain it. I'm sure many of you have heard the pastoral illustration about boiling a frog. If you put a frog in a pot of boiling water, his toes are barely going to hit that 212-degree water before he's jumped right back out of it. However, if you put him in the cool water and start warming it with him in it, he will just enjoy the spa until he's cooked. This is the same idea. The person being abused steps into a loving relationship, cool water. Then the heat begins slowly, barely noticeable, but it is there. The temperature rises and grows until she's fully cooked—his words are baked into her psyche as truth.

Abuse has several faces, and every single one of them is ugly. Whether it's a degrading comment or a slap, it damages. It kills the spirit, and it destroys the soul—of both people involved. It is also a major sin. Seriously, God said we are to encourage and lift each other up. He said a man is to love his wife as himself. Abuse does neither of those.

Whew! That's some heavy reading, huh? I don't have much tongue-in-cheek stuff to say about this topic. I can't tell you why God said to write it, other than He and I have discussed it at length. I've come a long way from the time when I thought I was "short, fat, and ugly" and that I was someone's "plump little pigeon" or that my opinions didn't matter anyway. Now I stand on the side of survivor. I've faced a horrible disease, and I've lived through it. I have a lot of battle scars, though. Maybe that's what I'm supposed to share. Just as the surgery for melanoma left scars on my body, abuse left scars on my heart and in my mind. It has also fueled passions deep inside me to help those who might be headed down the same path.

But wait, didn't I just say that the abused wouldn't hear? Yeah, I did. But just like people possibly not hearing when we share the Gospel doesn't change our command to share it, having a girl ignore my warnings about a new boyfriend or having a woman brush off my attempts to help doesn't change that gnawing desire in me to help them, to share the truth.

I think it is the same with anything we live through. If we will look for the good that comes from it, we will find that God will use it to help others.

So, if you are being abused, whether physically or emotionally, realize that it is not love. Realize that his words are not truth. Recognize that God made you the wonderful person He intended and that you have worth. God sees you as worth dying for. Determine to get help. If your relationship is one of marriage, I will not counsel you to divorce him, but I will suggest that you get away to someplace safe. Go someplace where you can get counseling and he can't get to you. God hates divorce, and He wants to see all the hurts mended; trust Him in that. Also know that physical separation isn't divorce. It is protection. It is help. It is safety. Trust God in that, too. While you are in that safe place, dive into Him. Drink His Word like it is water in the desert. Devour the Bible like a starving soul—you are. Let Him speak to your wounded heart and bring it life. Then let Him lead your next steps.

I can warn you ahead of time, forgiveness is one of those next steps. Yeah, He expects you to forgive even this. I've forgiven my ex-husband for all the words and all the hurt. I've forgiven him for the affairs and the lies. I'm not his buddy, but we were able to attend our son's graduation from the Air Force boot camp together, and then sit across from one another and enjoy lunch. Sometimes, when I think about the events that have gone on in our lives together, I wonder how much of what happened was borne from his own insecurities and misunderstanding of love. In the movie *Fireproof*, the main character is told that he can't love his wife because he doesn't understand what love is. I think there's a lot of truth in that, and my hope is that perhaps now, almost twenty years after our split, my ex-husband has finally healed and learned what love really is.

If you are abusing the person you say that you love, stop. Please, just stop. Whether it is words or fists or manipulation, just stop. Remember the movie *Bambi*? The baby rabbit was named Thumper. His mom had a rule for him to live by, apparently because he had problems with saying bad things about others. It was simple, "If you can't say somethin' nice, don't say nuffin' at all." The person you say you love is precious in God's sight—and so are you. Take some time to figure out why you can't say nice things to him or her. Learn what it is that causes you to do the things you do. God has so much more for you. Run to Him. Seek Him. Find out what it is He wants you to know to the deepest core of your being.

If you are on the outside looking in, pray. Seek God's help constantly. Ask Him to give you opportunities to speak truth into both lives, and then do it. Don't hate the abuser. He or she needs real love as much as the victim. He or she is reacting out of something he or she doesn't understand and we surely don't, but I believe he or she needs help and healing, too.

Finally, if you are a survivor—either an abuser or a victim of abuse, what are you doing with that experience now? As you learn and grow in your healing, do you share that with others, or do you hide it away unwilling to share that "weakness" about yourself? My hope is that you will open up and share your story, not to glorify you or to vilify your abuser, but to share how amazingly good God is and how His healing is real and ongoing, forever.

No Cover-ups

...admitting mistakes.

God, why can't people just say they made a mistake? Why can't they say they made a bad choice?

We love celebrities, don't we? We watch TV shows about them, read newspaper and magazine articles about them, celebrate weddings and births, and cry when they fall or fail.

Whether they are movie stars, TV stars, politicians, athletes, or talk show hosts, we tend to make them heroes. In the recent past, one bad-boy Major League Baseball player did a big no-no. When asked how he thought that wrongdoing would affect the millions of children who looked up to him, his answer was that he didn't ask to be their hero and what he did was his business. Well, that sparked talk show commentary for weeks! In my humble—okay, not so humble—opinion, parents are responsible for directing their children's attention to good and real heroes and for explaining that these heroes are people, just like them. They are heroes because they have stepped past their life, their limitations, and their fears to do what is good and right.

They're not that hard to find. Look at New York City on September 11, 2001. When people fled from the World Trade Center Towers, we watched firefighters, paramedics, and police personnel run *toward* those same towers.

When the two crazed gunmen—boys—killed many of their peers at Columbine High School, they asked some of those students if they believed in God before shooting them. At least one said yes. He or she is a hero.

Most recently, at Virginia Tech a seventy-six-year-old professor, a Holocaust survivor, gave his life holding the door to his classroom closed against a madman long enough for students to escape. He is a hero.

Let's get closer to home. Read your newspaper—was there a fire recently? Let's show our children the men and women who rushed into the burning building to be sure everyone was safely out. Let's visit these heroes in their grief when they deal with being unable to get to everyone in a fire or an accident.

Let's guide our children to understand that a hero is not someone who uses their God-given talents to make lots of money that they then spend on drugs, promiscuous sex, and alcohol. Let's show them that a true hero is one who gives completely of themselves in the service of others.

Heroes are people we want to emulate. Do we want to be just like that foul-speaking, tobacco-spitting, drug-glorifying athlete/

singer/actor that the world adores? Or do we want to start a revolution and be different?

Do we want to give our money to someone who advocates random sex and drug use? When our kids ask for "those" shoes or "that" shirt, find out why they like that person; learn for yourself the character of that person. If he or she is not someone you want your child to grow into, deny their request. Show them better choices, but don't give in. It is your job to guide them.

So, what happens when a hero or a celebrity falls? Immediately they are thrust into the limelight. The American media exists to give us every sordid detail of who the person is and what was done as well as to call in a pack of brilliant legal and psychological minds to figure out why they did it and what should be done to or by them.

Can you say nationwide soap opera?

We then get to see how these people deal with their mistakes and, all too often, see those mistakes blamed on others.

"My parents spanked me."

"My parents didn't love me."

"My teachers didn't teach me."

The list goes on and on, *ad nauseum*.

Whatever happened to standing there and admitting that you messed up? That you made a bad choice? Have we given up entirely on the notion of personal responsibility? We can't. Seriously, we can't.

On the flip side, when did it become our job to take on responsibility for everything? When did it become our job to be everything to everyone, perfect in every way? It's not.

There's a side to this that is wholly sad. The concept of being perfect has infiltrated our churches. Those who grew up as preachers' kids know very well what I'm talking about. They feel like they're under a microscope, being viewed by everyone and chastised by some for their behavior, as if being a pastor's child makes them immune to normal childlike behaviors.

Here's the thing, though. Romans 3:23 says, "All have sinned." It does not say, "All *but* the church leadership." We are all the same. While God does hold teachers and leaders to a higher standard, He never said they wouldn't or couldn't make mistakes. What He did say is they receive tougher judgment, harsher consequences (see James 3:1–2a). James even says, "We all stumble in many ways."

I feel this is a place where we fail one another in the church. We are called to make disciples. That means investing our lives in others, showing them right living, teaching them how to study the Bible, and how to be perfect.

Not!

It does mean investing our lives. It does mean *showing* them right living—including how to deal with our own mistakes. We must do that if we are to fulfill Jesus' edict in John 13:35. If we truly love someone, we don't let him or her continue in sin; we confront the person. The trouble is if we have never shown this person how to handle that situation, how will they know how to react in a godly way?

When we mess up, screw up, foul up, or whatever else you want to call it, we need to admit it. Confess. Agree with the truth.

Simply say, "I messed up," or "I made a bad choice." If someone brought it to your attention, thank them for that then apologize to anyone who was hurt by that choice and seek his or her forgiveness. If someone else is involved, go to them and seek their forgiveness. Let others see this, and finally, go to anyone you are helping to grow in their faith to apologize and ask forgiveness.

Is it embarrassing? Sure it is. Is it painful? Not physically, but it can break your heart. However, by doing this, you will glorify the Father and you will teach someone else the right way to rectify a problem.

The thing is, our mess-ups are messes. We'd rather just cover them up, never see them, and not let others see them. We'd rather keep up the façade that we are perfect. When we do that, though, young Christians never learn true humility, accountability, or forgiveness.

I'm not saying we should go before the church for every boo-boo. That takes the focus off of God and puts it on us, or worse, on the problem.

What I am advocating is allowing others to see and hear us go to someone and quietly, humbly offer an apology and seek forgiveness. No details are necessary, as those involved already know them.

There is currently a commercial on TV for an insurance company that starts out with a man picking up a child's toy from a crowded sidewalk and returning it to the child. Next, that child's mother moves a man's coffee cup to keep it from falling off the table. A man who sees her helps a man who fell on a wet sidewalk. A man who witnessed that act then holds an elevator for someone. Another man notices and keeps a driver from backing over a motorcycle while parking. The woman who sees that then prevents a co-worker from falling. Another co-worker observes that, sees boxes about to fall on a man on a busy street, and runs to pull him out of the way. A man who sees her then kindly waves someone out into a busy traffic jam in front of him. Another driver sees it and is later jogging, when he stops to retrieve a child's toy as the father watches. This father is the original nice person.

I find this a wonderful example of how every tiny thing we do touches the lives of others for a long time, even changing lives.

Scripture is filled with such examples. Church people call it Christ-like behavior. What it reveals, if we look closely, is the fact that no matter how right or wrong our action or reaction, someone is watching, someone sees.

What we do, more than what we say, will be emulated, repeated, and grown.

So, now comes the hard question. Who's got a problem with you? Okay, so you didn't do anything to make them mad, but they are. Now's the time. Matthew 5:23–24 says you need to do it even before you try to worship. "It" is you going to that person to apologize for hurting them or offending them and asking for his or her forgiveness. Since Jesus says to lay your offering down, take care of the relationship, and then come back to the offering, it would seem that He considers that "it" important.

Wonder why He said leave your offering there at the altar? Could it be that He meant for others to see us doing what He requires? Could it be that He knew if we came to a place of worship while still harboring conflict in our hearts, His Holy Spirit would move in our hearts to remind us of this relationship problem? That others would see the problem? That others already knew? Could it be that Christ expects us to be open and honest and humble enough to allow others to see that we are not perfect, but that there *is* a godly way to handle things?

Think on that a while.

Looking again at personal responsibility, whatever happened to saying, "I messed up, please forgive me?" It seems to have been replaced with excuses and shifting of blame.

I distinctly remember having the comptroller of the company that I kept inventory records for come to me in an absolute tizzy. He stated the problem, showed me the discrepancy, then asked me how on Earth that had happened.

Pause a moment!

This was a perfect chance to discuss the incompetence of those reporting their data to me, their lack of procedural ethics, the fallacy of their counts, and the ineptitude of those taking the inventory.

Trouble is my job was to be that last line of defense. If there were a question or delay in reporting, it was my job to call and expedite the procedure. If they weren't producing reports according to policy, it was my job to train, retrain, train again, and, if necessary, involve management to correct the issue. If the counts were wrong, it was my job to question them. It was never my job to pass along incorrect information.

That meant I had only one response available to me.

Unpause.

I stated simply, "I messed up. I'm sorry. I'll go back over it and bring you the corrected version as soon as possible."

The tirade was over. Mr. Comptroller couldn't speak. He was so used to hearing excuses that when given a sincere answer accepting responsibility, he didn't know what to say. I actually smiled as I watched him turn and walk back to his office speechless. I had to work hard to suppress a giggle as he disappeared through the doorway.

Next time you've made a mistake, own up to it. No excuses. Just own it.

On the other hand, if someone compliments you, accept it. Don't dismiss it; just say thank you and move on. False humility is just as bad as passing blame and making excuses.

Don't Wait

...apologies.

*But God, I wasn't wrong, was I? Why do I have to say
I'm sorry?*

Apologies hurt. Admitting we've been wrong about something
stings. We think that shows weakness, and we certainly don't want
to appear weak.

Thing is, apologies hurt briefly. That thing left unapologized for
hurts forever.

My first marriage ended in divorce, the result of his multiple
affairs. I hurt horribly. Then I married a wonderful man with two
sons. I made my only-child son a middle-child son—if anyone can
warp a kid, that's me.

The thing is, I came into this relationship as a woman hurt on
so many levels and was thrust into motherhood times three. My
mind told me that it was my job to shape these boys into men, and
my damaged heart lost the battle to love them and simply hung

onto rules and laws, and you'd better not break them—even the smallest one. A modern-day Pharisee, that was me.

My eldest stepson is an amazing guy. The first time I met him, he sat on the kitchen counter and told me jokes. I laughed. They were good. His dad told me later that he'd said that he liked me because I laughed at his jokes. What that poor fellow went through when his father and I married! The woman who laughed at his jokes became a shrewish lawgiver with little mercy.

My son struggled with his new position in the family. I was his mom, but he now had to share me, and he didn't like that. In my mind, I simply *had* to show favor to the other two, because they were so ravaged by things their own mother had done. And thus I ravaged the emotions of my own son.

The youngest lived with us the longest and has seen the changes in me, but he's seen the worst, too. In time, I stopped the lawgiving. No, I changed the lawgiving. I realized the love God has for me. I let Him come in and heal places that I'd closed the door on, hoping to never deal with those things again. And in that healing, God had changed me.

Recently, as I was praying for that eldest boy, now a thirty-year-old husband, father, and foreman on a job he's thrived in for almost ten years, God spoke to my heart, telling me I had to apologize to him.

I what?

I kinda argued with God because it had been so long, and it would bring up old wounds and bad memories and all those excuses we are so good at devising. You know what? God didn't budge. So, I shared with a few good friends what my "assignment" was. That was for accountability. I'd hear from them, asking me what I'd done to complete my assignment, and I knew they were praying for both me and my stepson.

Finally, on Thanksgiving Day 2008, I pulled him outside from the rest of the family and read the letter I'd written him. I cried a ton of tears, and he listened quietly to every word. He gave me forgiveness that I needed, and we talked—like adults—about adult and family things like we've never done before. God's up to something with that boy—er, man.

That's *my* story. What's yours? Have you done something that was so mean and so incredibly stupid that it has destroyed a relationship completely? Or was it something completely unintentional that has changed a relationship, made it something less than it once was?

Apologize.

Yep. Do it. Again, the words of Jesus in Matthew 5:23–24 come to mind: "So if you are presenting a sacrifice at the altar in the Temple and you suddenly remember that *someone has something against you*, leave your sacrifice there at the altar. Go and be reconciled to that person. Then come and offer your sacrifice to God" (emphasis mine).

Apologies seem to mean a lot in God's definition of relationship.

Don't know what it was that you did? Ask God to tell you. He knows. And if you're not patient enough to wait on God, ask that person. Go to them in an attitude of true humility and sorrow, and ask them what you've done to harm them, to break their heart. They might not tell you, but they will see your heart, if you are honest with them.

And if they do tell you, don't go getting all puffed up and defensive and proceed to tell them how you had the right to do that thing. The idea is that you are seeking restoration of the relationship with that person.

Oh, here's a news flash: You may never get that relationship back. The hurt may be more than that person can handle, but you do need to make that apology, and with the Spirit's leading. And here's an idea: Next time, let's not wait so confounded long before we make it.

Deal?

You Can't Make Me Mad

...control. Who gets it?

Lord, why do people blame others for their own reactions? Why do we let others control our emotions?

Parents, do you remember asking one of your children why he or she fought with someone only to hear, "He made me so mad!"

Employers hear it, law enforcement officers hear it, and society is rife with it.

I believe anger is an emotion. I also believe it is a choice. Paul says in Ephesians 4:26 to be angry but to not sin. That doesn't seem like an uncontrolled or uncontrollable emotion, does it?

The fact is any emotion is a reaction to a situation or circumstance around us. Of course, the easiest thing to do is to not think things through and let our emotions reign, free of considered thought. Then we can just use that well-worn phrase, "He (she) just ticked me off!" or whatever version you prefer.

In reality, the easiest thing (and the hardest thing) is to think. Just because a situation is at a high level of intensity doesn't mean that we have to have rapid-fire answers. We can slow down and consider our response before we share it.

How many times are those high stress levels we endure actually self-inflicted? I was working an office job about thirty minutes from home. For the longest time, I'd find myself banging on the steering wheel, saying some rather unflattering things about other drivers who obviously did not know or care that I needed to get my self-important ego to my desk to get to work. They didn't seem to grasp that they were in my way, and they just needed to *get off the road* and *let me by*. Arriving at my destination, pulling into the parking lot almost on two wheels, and skidding to a stop in the last parking space did little to begin my day pleasantly.

I finally realized that my stress was self-inflicted. When I realized that leaving home just ten minutes earlier would put me ahead of most of that traffic as well as give me a buffer, the steering wheel sighed (I'm sure I heard it!) with gratitude. I made a better choice.

The situation changed little. I still had to drive thirty minutes. I was still faced with some drivers who refused to recognize my need for speed. What changed was my reaction. The only one who could change that was me.

I think that many times when we choose anger as a reaction, we direct it at others when, in reality, we ourselves should be the recipients. In my previous story, my anger was at myself for *my* slowness in getting ready or my choice to hit that snooze button one time too many. That didn't keep me from displaying it to others, and it didn't lower my stress level.

So, anger is a choice, a reaction. What about happiness? Yep, it's a choice, too. As believers in Christ, we are given joy as a fruit of the Spirit of God living in us, but what I'm talking about is being happy. Joy is a gift, a state, a reality for the child of God, just like patience. Being happy is our choice, our decision.

Here's a disclaimer right off the bat: Yes, there are people who have problems with depression, and I am not saying that is their choice. I've been there, and though I did not buy the ticket for that trip, I went anyway. Thankfully, God walked with me through it, and although it is still a struggle at times, it is not my daily battle. I'm sure that some of you who are reading my words (thank you, by the way) are under the care of a physician and perhaps on medication for depression. I applaud you. My only request is that you don't let your Xanax or Prozac or other drug become the only way you deal with life. Being numb isn't dealing with it.

What I'm talking about is that situation you're in. What is it? A job you don't like? Living with people who irritate you? Going to school? Going to jail? Whatever your situation, you have the choice to be happy there. Not necessarily happy *with* the situation, but happy regardless of the situation.

I was mother of a two-month-old son with a husband fresh out of EMT training and no job. We were living in a trailer that his parents had bought, in a fish camp in Florida. During my pregnancy, I'd tried my hand being a Tupperware lady but didn't make enough to call it a living. We needed to do something, and I found a job at a small local college working in their bulk mail room.

It wasn't what I called fun, dropping my baby off to go to work in a very intense workplace, but that's where I was and what was needed. I made the choice to be happy there. Now mind you, not even two years prior, I'd been working, making more than double the wage with better benefits and in a place that was much more fun. Still, happiness was my choice in this job in this place. Why be miserable? I didn't see any benefit in that, so I would kiss my son as I dropped him off with my mother, thank her for keeping him, and continue on to my job. I worked to learn all I could while I was there, taking joy in every accomplishment.

Later, living in a state over 600 miles from home and family, I learned to be happy in spite of trying financial times, a poor work situation, and learning that my husband had a girlfriend. Oh, trust me, I had plenty of down and depressed times, too. Angry times. Downright spiteful times. Mean and vengeful times. Then I would realize that my happiness would not result from my job or my husband's fidelity, or lack thereof, or even from striking it rich. I knew I had to find my happiness where I could every day. So, I looked for it.

I found it in watching my son enjoy his first real autumn, rolling down a hill into a pile of leaves, only to jump up and run to the top and do it over again, his face beaming.

I found it in meeting people at work and learning ways to help them, even if it was just with a smile.

I found it in returning to my faith, going back to the One who never failed me.

I found it in watching snow pile up to three feet then sledding on it—something a girl from Florida doesn't grow up doing.

Happiness dwells all around us. Sometimes we find it then lose it, because we don't choose to hang onto it or we think it requires something or someone else. We choose our focus, and so many times. we choose poorly.

So, what's your situation? Where are you right now? Is your marriage crumbling? Your finances dwindling? Your kids on the edge? Your health waning? Choose happiness. Choose to make changes for your marriage, choose to use the money better, and choose to hold your kids, love them, and teach them to soar.

God said a merry heart is good medicine. Perhaps the only happiness you can muster right now is that you still have a roof over your head, even if it isn't your own and isn't much of a roof. Revel in it. Don't look at any flaws or the places that need repair. Don't look at how it measures up to so-and-so's house. Rejoice in those walls. They protect you from the elements. Be happy that you have that.

See your children? Be happy for them. See what they smile at, watch their wonder, and recapture your happiness through that.

You see now how our emotions are not in charge of us? We must be in charge of them. To be otherwise is to be under the control of the one pushing our emotional buttons.

I want to be clear on this. We all have emotions. We feel certain things based on our circumstances or situation. My contention is, however, that no one else *makes* us feel this way or that, and no one ever causes our reactions. That is completely our choice. I think we do far too much reacting and not nearly enough thinking.

There was a story in the local news recently. It seems this man's wife was having an affair with a much younger man, so the husband shot and killed the young man. To me this case was all about choices. I don't know the people or all of the details of the case, but let's just let our minds wander a bit. Please understand, some of these are not the facts that came out during the trial, but the understanding is the same.

Wife is feeling unloved and undervalued.

Husband loves wife, but isn't very demonstrative or vocal about it.

The Other Man sees wife as beautiful and tells her so.

Wife is flattered and drawn to Other Man and...

Stop! Here's one of those choice-making moments. Wife must choose between keeping her vows and starting a relationship with Other Man.

Stop again! Other Man knows she is married. He must choose whether to just give her the compliment then move on or press forward toward an intimate relationship.

Other Man asks Wife out.

Wife begins meeting Other Man for dinner and then moves into intimacy.

Other Man begins feeling deeper emotions for Wife.

Wife and Other Man begin meeting at her home when Husband is gone.

Husband realizes something is going on, asks questions, argues with Wife, learns of the affair, and sulks.

Stop! Choice time! Husband finds out his wife is intimate with another man, in their home no less. His emotions are all over the place, running the gamut from shock and disbelief to fear to anger to hurt.

He has a choice right now: Leave the home to give him and his wife time apart, send her away, give her a choice between him and the other man, or seek her forgiveness for failing her and ask that they work on their marriage.

Stop! Wife now has a choice to make based on Husband's. (Keep up; this can get hard to follow!)

If he chooses to leave, Wife must choose to put away her lover and seek reconciliation with Husband or call Other Man and invite him over.

If he chooses to toss her out, Wife must choose where to go— to a friend's house, hotel, shelter, or her lover.

If he tells her to choose between him and Other Man, Wife must choose to accept his terms to work on their marriage and put Other Man on the road, or she must choose to go to Other Man, leaving her marriage and all that went with it.

If he seeks her forgiveness and asks that they work on their marriage, she must choose whether to grant that forgiveness — talk with him about her hurts and listen to his and work with him to grow their marriage back to life—or whether to deny him forgiveness and continue her relationship with Other Man.

Wife continues her relationship with Other Man.

Husband sulks and stews.

Other Man parks outside Husband and Wife's home and waits for Husband to leave so he can go in.

Stop! Do I have to go over the different choices they each could have made here?

Husband goes to his gun rack and takes down a shotgun that he borrowed from someone, making sure it is loaded, and then walks out to the car where Other Man waits.

Other Man dies. Husband goes to jail. Wife mourns—alone.

People, this was the last poor choice. Husband could have told his wife to go to Other Man and not come back, changed the locks, and gone on living. Now he sits in a cell, awaiting his trial for murder. Some argue that it is justified, while others call it premeditated. My point is, it was all about choices, and at any given time, a different choice *could* have been made that would have left Other Man alive and Husband free. Perhaps none of the three would have been the happiest people on the planet with the others' choices, but they would all three be alive and free.

There is much more to this story. It all came out in a trial that had the community at odds for weeks. That doesn't negate the fact that it was a string of poor choices resulting in the death of a young man and changed lives all around.

Most of our everyday choices aren't that life altering—or are they? When we choose to live, even for a moment, outside God's will, who will it hurt?

Paul said to the Thessalonians to avoid even the appearance of evil (1 Thessalonians 5:22). Wow, that's harsh—seems kinda legalistic.

Guess that means we can't be around drug dealers or prostitutes, can't walk into a place of gossip. Better not go to a buffet—too much gluttony there. Take it to the extreme, will you?

God most definitely wants us *in* those places. He tells us to be a light, shining in the dark—rather hard to see a light shining in the midst of other lights. I believe Paul was saying to these people who lived in that major harbor city to not be like those who walked in darkness.

See, some of the people there had heard the gospel and accepted Christ. Then Paul later got word that they had taken some of his preaching and teachings to the extreme. (We haven't changed much in 2,000 years, huh?) He had told them that Jesus would return one day and that they were to be watchful, waiting upon His return. Well, those goofy church people got together and discussed that and decided that Paul left out the fact that the "one day" was soon, very soon, and that he meant to say "be watching." So, they decided to be watching. Many ceased their work, even their daily chores, to sit and watch the sky.

This is what can be called a conundrum (a question or problem having only a conjectural answer; an intricate and difficult problem). Yes, we should always be watchful. That's different from watching. It is wrong to cease doing what God has given us to do even if it is done in order to watch for Christ's return.

That's what Paul was telling those folks at Thessalonica. He wanted them to be watchful, yet to not be like the sinners or evildoers who did nothing to grow God's kingdom. He didn't want them to even be seen doing what the sinners or evildoers do.

So, here's your modern-day application of that principle. Certainly go to the prostitutes—go in pairs, to prevent it from appearing that you're going to solicit. Go there, take them some coffee, maybe something nutritious to eat, but don't dress like them, don't lean into cars like them. Be a light. Share with them the hope that lies within you. Love them like Christ does, and tell them how much God values them, just because they are who they are. He doesn't hate them because of what they do. He's not happy with their lifestyle, but He is still crazy in love with them.

Likewise where drugs are dealt and used. Take a friend—it is moral, emotional, spiritual, and physical protection. Don't go to any of these people and berate their lifestyle. Jesus only did that with the religious people. Go to them with love and hope, being willing to share the grace of God with those who, for whatever reason, are cast aside from society.

Here is one admonition to remember in this endeavor, though. When you go, when you share, especially in these places of the darkest night, don't be alarmed or disappointed if the people just turn away. Even Paul knew that he was a seed-sower. He knew there were others who would water and feed until others would harvest. We are to sow seed…or water…or harvest. It may be different in every situation. You just have to be ready for any of those, and know that you are doing what God has said for you to do; He will bless it and use it as *He* wills.

There was a drought in the southeastern United States the summer and fall of 2008. Not knowing it was on its way, we faithfully went out in the spring and placed seed in the ground.

I don't know if you've ever planted a home garden, but I find it a fitting example for this principle I just mentioned. To plant corn, for example, you hew out a small hole and drop in three or four kernels of seed corn—not just one! Then you cover it, fertilize it, and water it. Later, up from the ground rises a (one, singular) stalk, stretching toward heaven to produce food and more seed.

Normally.

Generally.

However, a drought changes things drastically. The seeds were planted. For a time they received water. They sprouted, and the stalks grew. They appeared to produce the food and seed as expected.

…as normally occurs.

…as generally happens.

However, this season, seed plus minimal water produced nothing. No roasting ears. No corn on the cob. No creamed corn. Nothing.

Here's your application of this principle. Someone has planted a tiny seed or two, and then you come along. God hands you a watering can. You sprinkle a dab of it around and see a miracle.

Sprouts emerge from the hard ground, and you set that watering can down—after all, you've done what you were called to do, right? The growth stops. There is no harvest.

This is why it is crucial that we be ready at all times to share the reason for the hope that lies within us. See 1 Peter 3:15.

St. Francis of Assisi is credited with saying, "Preach the Gospel always; if necessary use words." What a powerful edict! I believe he got it. He realized that living his life in front of others was just as important, if not more so, as the words he preached.

The same is true with us. What happens to what a person expresses as God's truth when that person is observed in the next small town getting drunk and loving on someone who isn't their spouse? Sadly, not only is that person's reputation damaged, the body of Christ is as well. Worse yet, the words of truth that he (or she) may have shared are tossed aside as so much garbage.

By the same token, a person can live his life in such a way that people experience love, kindness, forgiveness, and peace and never hear him preach; yet they see God.

I don't believe that living it is enough, though. I believe our life gives credence to our words. It validates what we say we believe, but we are still not relieved of the duty given to us by God to tell people about His incredible crazy love for them.

GOD LOVES A SMART-ALEC

...being real.

Lord, why did you make me with the wit You did? Why is the
quick retort, play-on-words reply so natural to me? I've been told
that it's irreverent and wrong. Is it?

God doesn't smite us or kill us or strike us down when we get
all smart-alec-y with Him. Seriously. Read the eleventh chapter of
Numbers. The people whined. The outsiders that, for whatever
reason, had decided to travel with Israel whined and agitated the
Israelite whining. Then Moses whined—no, Moses got downright
smart with God. Hear the tone of his voice; see the stance of his
body as he speaks to God:

And Moses said to the LORD, 'Why are you treating me,
your servant, so harshly? Have mercy on me! What did I do
to deserve the burden of all these people? Did I give birth
to them? Did I bring them into the world? Why did you tell
me to carry them in my arms like a mother carries a nursing
baby? How can I carry them to the land you swore to give
their ancestors? Where am I supposed to get meat for all

these people? They keep whining to me, saying, 'Give us meat to eat!' I can't carry all these people by myself! The load is far too heavy! If this is how you intend to treat me, just go ahead and kill me. Do me a favor and spare me this misery!' (Numbers 11:11–15 NLT)

The next verse is *not* "and God smote Moses dead in His anger."

Obviously, as a mother, I needed to learn this and my mother before me, because if I got my anger up and said things like this to my mama, I'd be busted for sure. The last time was when I was sixteen years old.

Instead, God gives Moses help: seventy of the nation's elders and leaders. Of course, part of this meant that some of the Spirit that was given to Moses had to be shared with those seventy, but God gave him the help he requested.

Now what do we learn from this?

First of all, we learn that God isn't bothered by our emotions. He knows how we feel and think. Sometimes He knows something we don't—He can put a finger on what the problem is when we don't have a clue.

We can understand that God loves us completely, no matter what we do or say. Even if we ball up our fist and raise it to the sky, a la Scarlett O'Hara, or put our hands on our hips and fuss. He's okay with it and loves us anyway.

I believe God loves the honest expression of our feelings to Him—read the Psalms. I also think we'd save tons of money on counseling if we would grasp that concept. Not that getting counseling is bad—been there, done that. Sometimes we need someone who will talk back and aim us toward the right thinking. However, if we could get to the place where we could look to God and say what we are thinking, we'd be so much better off.

I was recently challenged by a book, *Crazy Love* by Francis Chan. Amazing guy. He hit me square between the eyes when he talked about how we think about the people around us. That if we are going to love like Jesus, we even have to love the guy who cuts in front of us in traffic. Didn't we talk about this earlier? Anyway, I had read that portion of the book in the morning, and not even eight hours later, I was cut off in traffic—very rudely, mind you. The driver of the truck had to have seen the sign telling him that his lane was ending, yet he continued to drive next to me. Sure enough, when the lane began to end—not where the stripes began telling him it was going to end, but when his lane ceased to exist—he sped up just enough to pop that big old truck with the huge bumper right into the lane, barely in front of me!

My initial reaction was to fuss. No, I didn't wave at him with one finger. I just started fussin' to God. Then He spoke directly into my heart the very words I'd read earlier that Francis Chan had written. I tried to pray for that man. Then I did something I've never done before. Alone in my car, I yelled aloud at God. I shook my fist. I said something like, "God! This is *so* not easy! I don't want to pray nice things for him. I don't want to love him. I want him to know how angry I am at what he's done."

And you know what? Right after that, my heart was broken for that man. I prayed for his home, his family, and him in a way that I never would have otherwise. And I lived through it. I think God honored my honesty. And He taught me something through it.

He taught me that life isn't all about me. He taught me that I can share every thought, even the bad ones with Him. He taught me that He can take it. He can take my despicable, hateful things and make them beautiful, if I give them to Him.

He has also taught me something about this smart alec thing. I have a reasonably quick wit—sometimes. It's usually better after coffee. I've told others that, for some reason, God's given me a brain that retains a zillion bits of information, even if I haven't studied it. I'm a whiz at Trivial Pursuit. I've often called it "retention of random bits of useless information," but I've also learned that it is only useless until someone needs it. Then (bam!) it is brought up out of the recesses of my memory to serve. However, there are times that what those bits of information do are surface to allow me to converse.

Smart alec or sarcastic banter is my forte. I'm good and comfortable with that. When things get too heavy or intimate, it sprouts up. Sometimes, it is good. Other times, it's not so good.

God's working on me to know when to put it out there and when to just "shutteth up." (That's the King James Version, you know.)

My point is: God is the one who gave me this sense of humor and wit—has to be. Neither of my parents is gifted with it—their gifts are more relational. Mother is kind and loving; Dad's never met a stranger—even at a gas station a thousand miles from home, often to my total embarrassment.

What strange gifts has God planted in you? Humor? Out-of-the-park creativity? Storytelling? Drama? Painting? Dance? Whatever it is, don't assume that it is not something God wants to use. He's put that in you for a reason. He has a specific purpose for your life, and your personality is a part of that. It might seem abnormal to you, but to God, it is just what He planned. Don't extinguish it! Delight in it! Be excited that God picked *you* for that. Then spend some time finding out how and where God wants to use it.

Oh yes, there is a disclaimer to this: You don't get to just let that gift run willy-nilly through life. Everything you do or say affects other people, whether its family, friends, or even strangers. Even though I tend to use it sometimes, there is not a spiritual gift of bluntness or sarcasm. That's where the moment-by-moment relationship with Jesus comes in again. When you spend time with Him, even the smart alec side of you can be used for His holy purposes.

Conversations with a Cynic

...answering well.

Oh for Pete's sake! Where does he come up with such ideas and opinions? How can I argue with that? What on earth do I say? Should I even bother? God, help me!

Have you ever run across someone who doesn't believe the things that you do? They might believe some of what you do but challenge you on others.

What do you do with them? Do you argue with them, working intently to make them see things the "right" way—your way? Do you even listen to what they have to say? Do you dismiss their questions as too ridiculous to bother with?

Or do you listen? Do you hear their heart? Do you let their questions soak into that place where God lives in you? Do you mull over what they are asking? Do you tell them their questions and opinions are valid and reasonable?

Having these kinds of conversations is not easy. None of us like to have our beliefs challenged. But allow me to posit this: They *should* be challenged, and regularly.

Just recently, I sat in a conference where Josh McDowell challenged teens and adults alike with the question, "Is it wrong to lie" When the room responded with a resounding, "Yes!" his response was, "Why?" He then challenged those reasons offered, ranging from what parents have taught to being in the Bible.

Part of his concept was difficult for many to grasp. There were many dropped jaws and gasps of disbelief as he told us not to believe something is right or wrong just because it was written in the Bible. He went on to explain that morals and rightness/wrongness are determined based on the nature and character of God, and anything that is contrary to that is wrong. For example, God is love, so anything contrary to love is wrong. God is truth, so anything contrary to truth is wrong.

My point in sharing this is not to regurgitate Josh McDowell's teaching, but to challenge your thinking. Why do you believe what you believe? Why do you believe in going to church on Sunday? It's not the original Sabbath, you know.

Why do you believe, or not believe, in tithing?

Why do you believe what you do about pastors or deacons or elders or church buildings or missions?

What do you believe about abortion? Why?

What do you believe politically? Why?

I ask you to examine those and more, because one day, you will meet up with a cynic. That person, given the opportunity, will challenge your thinking, your beliefs, and even your motives.

I think many people, Christians especially, regard their beliefs as being the only right way to believe.

Now don't get messed up on me here, there are tons of things that only have one answer, that's God's. What I'm saying is more about people's opinions and beliefs. For example, it is my belief that Coca-Cola makes the best soft drinks. That's my opinion, but I have a friend who believes just as strongly that if it is not Pepsi, it is not worth drinking. Neither of us is wrong. We have our reasons.

And here is the irrefutable truth: That is not an essential. By essential I mean something upon which your eternity rests.

While Benjamin Franklin said that the only things certain in life are death and taxes, scripture says the one certain thing in life is death and, after that, the judgment. Have you seen Hebrews 9:27? It says, "Each person is destined to die once and after that comes judgment." Furthermore, we are told there's only one way to pass that judgment: acceptance of Jesus Christ as your Lord and Savior. *That* is essential.

Obviously there are further commands of Jesus to believers that we should most definitely obey, but most of the stuff we argue about is just stuff.

Dunk or sprinkle? As long as you've accepted Jesus as your Savior, I don't care.

Predestined or full grace? As long as Jesus is your Savior, I'm cool with either one.

Pre-tribulation, mid-tribulation, post-tribulation? As long as you have a moment-by-moment relationship with Jesus Christ, it's cool—you'll be upset whichever one it is if you don't know Him!

Here's a thought I've shared with numerous others—and I get mixed reviews and opinions on. I can best explain it, I think, with an example.

In the mountains of East Tennessee, chainsaw carvings have become a big thing. I find it an amazing craft, because all I can make with a chainsaw is sawdust!

A local artisan has chosen to get attention for his art by creating some pieces that he finds attractive or that speak to him—as any artist does. They range from a black bear using a urinal—a real urinal—to two bears mating, to a nearly-naked woman laying forward on what appears to be a flying or speeding motorcycle. Personally, I'm warped enough to think the bathroom bear is funny.

A bear standing in front of a urinal, looking back over his shoulder, yeah, to me that's funny. I'm not going to buy it, but it's funny.

There are some who have come to me saying we should do something to shut him down and get rid of the offensive art. Imagine their shock when I won't help in their campaign. It is after all, the "Christian" thing to do. I contend that while that may be, it may not be the Christ-like thing to do—or even think.

Okay. Close your mouth. I'll explain.

The man creating these carvings is lost. Why on Earth would he act or think like a believer? Why would we expect him to not create art that he, in his lost state, enjoys and likes?

Are you slapping your forehead saying, "D'oh!" or are you looking at these words with the certainty that I've lost what little mind I used to have? That's okay. At least you are thinking now.

As believers in Christ, we believe that having that carving of a nearly-nude woman is offensive. There are probably as many reasons for that as there are people thinking it. I can agree that it is not something I personally find attractive or inspiring, which is what art should be. I believe that it ignites thoughts that can lead to sin, and I believe it belittles women—making them objects, less than people. That's me. That's my belief.

Mr. Carver-man, however, doesn't believe that way, and he doesn't believe in Christ as Savior. My job as a servant of Christ is not to make this man live within the moral boundaries that I do; my job is to do whatever it takes to lead this man to take his next step toward Christ. I'm supposed to love him, build a relationship with him, and let him see Christ in me. It is okay to tell him why I don't like this piece of art or that—we're sharing opinions; but it is just as wrong for me to insist he live by my morals— maybe even more so if that insistence prevents him from knowing Christ as Savior—as it could ever be to have a carved nude in one's front yard.

Have you thought about the one thing that angered the religious people about Jesus? It was the fact that rather than hang with them doing their church things, He went out and hung with the paupers, the sick, and the sinful. He even told the religious ones that He didn't come for those who were already well, those who believed, He was there for those who didn't believe. The Pharisees and other religious leaders knew they kept the Law and observed all the intricacies thereof. They knew that they were godly and were highly incensed that this man, this so-called Messiah, would call them sinners and go to parties with the ones who were unworthy to even enter the Temple.

So, next time you see that offensive thing, that despicable sign, that abhorrent place, how about getting to know the one behind it and leading them to the One you know who will meet every need they have, including ones they don't realize they have.

Jesus loved people in spite of their lost condition, their horrible morals, and their hateful attitudes, but He refused to hang out with those who thought their religious acts made them righteous.

Instead, He went out to those who knew how horribly wretched they were, and He touched them. He laughed with them. He loved them.

I read recently of a church that partnered with a Hooters restaurant to meet some of the needs of a community that had been devastated by a hurricane.

Wait. Isn't Hooters that restaurant where the waitresses are barely covered?

Yep. That's the one.

Well, it seems that an associate pastor of the local Baptist church met up with a young lady at a gas station. They talked briefly, and the young woman shared of her exhaustion after work, making it hard to get to church. This pastor gave her his business card, telling her to call him if she felt the need. Imagine his surprise to hear from the manager of the restaurant where the young lady worked a few days later, inviting the church staff and their spouses to dinner. That's right. The manager of the local Hooters invited the church staff in for dinner. He admits that they all pretty much kept their heads down that first time, but through repeat visits, where he took his Bible and his compassion, the employees of the restaurant began to feel valued. That sense was probably helped along by the goodies sent in by some of the senior adult church ladies.

The big news was, after Hurricane Ike, some of the Hooters waitresses heard about Oak Island. This island community off the Texas coast was almost completely destroyed by the 2008 storm. They learned that as December approached, the families on the island wouldn't have much of a Christmas, since they were living in tents and camper trailers. So, these hard-working, good-hearted servers asked the church to help pave the way for them to help. Between the church and the Hooters servers—yes, the Hooters Girls—four hundred people were fed hamburgers and chicken wings, and over $20,000 in gifts were distributed, including a sound system to replace the one that the local church on Oak Island had lost to Hurricane Ike.

Here's my question: Would you have talked to the waitress at the gas island? Would you have given her your business card? Would you take your spouse there to eat? The church staff?

There's nothing wrong with any of these. Oh, I know, we discussed it a little while ago. First Thessalonians says to "abstain from the very appearance of evil." Okay. So, what's evil about a Hooters restaurant? I'm trying to reconcile this with the fact that Jesus was caught attending dinner at the home of sinners, and He saw nothing wrong with it, even chastising the religious ones for thinking it inappropriate.

One quote from *The Baptist Standard* [4] that spoke volumes was from the manager of the restaurant to the pastor in their initial

---

4   The Baptist Standard, The Texas Baptist Newsjournal. George Henson, published
     January 11, 2009

phone conversation: "We're just looking for answers like anyone else." Brings back that word about being ready with an answer, doesn't it?

So, here's the first part of my challenge. Be the kind of believer that is readily recognizable as a believer. That is essential. Jesus said to be set apart and be different. The second part is to be approachable to unbelievers. Look people in the eye. Do not judge them for their dress or body art or place of employment. Just love 'em where they are.

That's it. They've got questions. You've got answers.

Your answers are useless if they can't approach you with their questions.

So, now, what's *your* next step? Dinner, anyone?

GET A CLUE!

...why the heck are you here?

Lord, you said to always be ready to answer the questions about
the hope in us as believers. I heard John-John, the homeless
man, say, "I don't know why the heck you're here." How do
I answer a question like that? And what if no one asks me
about my hope?

You've seen this reference several times in these pages. This
time, let's dive a bit deeper into it.

In 1 Peter 3:15, Peter wrote these words, "Instead you must
worship Christ as Lord of your life. And if someone asks you about
your Christian hope, always be ready to explain it."

He wrote those words right after speaking to the believers
about suffering for doing what is right. He basically gave them two
things to think about:

1. IF you do God's will and suffer for it, God *will* reward you.

2. Do NOT worry or be afraid of their threats.

This is where the "instead" comes in. The normal, natural tendency to being ridiculed and threatened when doing good things is to worry for one's life and well-being. God, through Peter, told His people to be *abnormal*, to be different and not worry about the suffering or the threats. By that strange behavior, people would wonder about how they could do that. How they could be teased, ridiculed, threatened and still respond without worry or fear. Then the natural tendency of the people's wonder would be to ask the question, "Why do you act like this?"

And that is precisely when we're to be prepared with the answer.

Are you?

Ready, I mean?

No? Well, let's study up.

Why don't you just go get that guy/girl who lied about you? You have every right!

How can you let them talk about you like that?

What are you going to do if they come after you?

You did all those nice things and they treat you like _____? You should just _____!

How do you answer?

Where's your hope?

The Amplified Bible says it this way, "Always be ready to give a logical defense to anyone who asks you to account for the hope that is in you."

These people asking the questions probably won't be believers, or they might be new in their faith. You can't expect to give them the stock-and-trade answer (the churchy answer). They will need to hear *why* you believe God is faithful. They will need to understand *how* He has provided for you in the past. They will need to hear truth and logic and reason, not just, "Well, that's what it says in the Bible."

So, think about it. What *is* your answer? Your "logical defense?"

But wait! There's more!

What if no one is asking you that kind of question?

That's a whole different kettle of fish. If you are not being asked about that difference in you, logic says they don't see any difference.

Ouch. That's harsh. It is also real, and I believe time is getting too short for us to tiptoe around this topic when people desperately need to know about the One who makes us different.

If they can't see a difference in us, then either there isn't one, or we need to do some polishing and growing.

If they're not asking, ask God why. If there is something in your life that is preventing them from asking, agree with God that there's a problem and make the necessary changes. Learn to live in such a way that the hope, the life, the joy, the love that lives in you begs an explanation.

Then be ready with that logical defense of your strange behavior. For some, their eternity could depend on it.

TYING THE BOW

...bringing it all together.

What does all this mean, Lord? Really, what does it mean to me?
In the everyday scheme of things, what does it mean?

We've covered a lot of ground here. Let's take just a minute to boil it all down. Actually, I think Jesus did that when He walked the Earth. He said that to love God with all your heart, soul, mind, and strength and to love others as yourself covers all the Law.

Wow. Really?

Just that simple?

Grief? If you are grieving, loving God with everything you are will help get you through. If you are helping someone who is grieving, loving them the way you want to be loved works. Simple.

Integrity? Be who God made you to be. Be true and honest. You wouldn't lie to God or want others to lie to you, right? Simple.

What people look like? Do you want others to talk about and judge the clothes you wear or the way you look? Simple.

Pleasing God? Love Him. Love others. Simple.

Taking Jonah trips? It is so much easier to just go and do what God says, right? Simple.

Patience is easy. You don't like to have horns honked at you for not seeing the green light appear, right? Grant that to someone else. Show what you'd like to have shown to you.

Abuse? Encouraging words are so much better, don't you think? Isn't that what you want? Simple.

Talking with cynics about your faith? You like it when people listen to your values and opinions, right? Simple.

All the other things we've covered are just that simple. Love God, love others as yourself. Loving Him is as easy as reading His Word to know what that looks like. Loving others as yourself might be a tad more difficult if you don't love yourself much, but think about how you long to be loved, that will help.

Love God with everything that you are. Wait. Isn't that just following all the rules again? What happened to grace? Let's think about that.

Look at the most love-filled relationship you know. It might be one of yours; it might be someone you know. Examine how the love works. Is that relationship built on rules? Probably not. Are there rules involved? Guidelines, perhaps.

What you likely see in a deeply loving relationship is two individuals choosing to love each other, regardless of anything. That love will be seen through acts of kindness toward the other, words of encouragement, and sacrifice. Sometimes one individual will sacrifice their plans or desires for the other, and then in the next instance, the other individual has turned from their wishes to give to the other.

Heart, soul, mind, strength. Someone in love, deeply in love, has that loved one deep in their heart and constantly on their mind. We will do all that our physical and emotional selves can do to share ourselves and our love with that person.

Our earthly relationships are the tiniest example of how we are to love God. First of all, it is a choice. We choose and decide, day in and day out, to love God. It may become as automatic as breathing, but it is a choice. The evidence is the same as with human relationships. Our hearts are full of love for Him, our thoughts of Him are constant, and our desire to please Him and be pleasing to Him fills our being.

When we love God this way, it will spill over to everyone we come in contact with.

So now, love God. Love others. Live simply and love extravagantly. It is truly within you.

ACKNOWLEDGEMENTS

First and foremost, I give all praise and honor and glory to God, Who has loved me despite the despicable mess I've been. He's pulled me out of messes galore and protected me from others. He is the reason for this book, He is the reason I live.

My husband, Jack Bryant, is the other reason this book is in your hands. While I kept saying, "someone should write about that," he heard God saying that the "someone" was me and told me that. Jack has been the physical example of the unconditional love of God. He loved the damaged soul that I was when we met and has loved me through everything since. Because of Jack, I have the confidence to strike out on this journey. *My life is richer because you are in it and I am so thankful that God placed you in my life, I love you more than words can begin to say. You've taught me, by example, what unconditional love looks like and how it feels. Knowing your love has helped me understand God's love better.*

The Cynic who challenged me, also named Jack, caused me to examine how I believed and why. He refused pat answers and caused me to think, not just react. It was through his challenges that many of the questions I've asked God came to be. Conversations with him have strengthened my understanding of God and life. *Your encouragement has strengthened my confidence and resolve, without your challenges, the words wouldn't be here on the page.*

Rhonda Wigington, good friend, confidante, woman I admire. She encourages and reins me in. She knows my flaws and loves me anyway. *Thank you for reading my book and sharing your life with me. Doing life with you is a trip! I wouldn't trade any of it for a bowl of potato soup!*

Darren Wigington, my pastor and good friend has been the example of being real in ministry. Through good and bad times, I've watched him live life authentically; living out what he says he believes. *My faith has grown because of your obedience to our God, and I value your honesty and the confidence you have in me more than you'll know. You're that brother I never had and I'm honored to call you friend. (And yes, I'll tithe on the profits of this book.)*

Jami Choy is another who has read these words providing commentary and suggestions and encouragement. She shares my lack of mercy and helps hold me in check with it. A young woman I am blessed to call my friend. *Jami, you ROCK – for a young whippersnapper, you're not bad.*

Julien Choy is Jami's husband who, along with Jami, has provided the place to write. The Coffee House in Townsend has become my "other office" where many of these words took shape. *You're wise beyond your years, young man, and I'm blessed to know you.*

Michelle Knoll is a friend I met because of Facebook and because I know people she knows – and that I fully believe God placed in my life. An author herself, Michelle took on the editing of these words, striving to make them make sense and read well. *I'm honored to now call you my friend and will ever treasure the prayers you've lifted on my behalf, please don't stop!*

Rich Willis, the high school friend who encouraged me way back when and continued doing so up until he went to Heaven just a few months before this book was published. *You're an amazing example of truth and grace, thank you for your friendship.*

Norma Johnson. *Thank you for speaking words of encouragement into my life for over ten years now. You've believed in me when I couldn't. You are a blessing to know.*

Greg Roberts, fellow church staff member who listens to my rants and changes my direction with a word. A man who lives on mission every minute of his life. *Thank you for being real and honest and for letting me be me. Your love for people has shown me how to love.*

Dottie Hall, a beautiful, Godly woman who knows where I've been, knows the challenges I face and often with just a look encourages me more than anyone can know. *Your love and understanding bless me and your faith challenges me. Thank you for being such an example to me.*

Michelle Roberts, my pixie-girl friend! *I love you dearly, and I know you love me, even though sometimes we're worlds apart. You do the shopping; I'll make your business cards. You style my hair and I'll give you props! You are talented in more ways than you believe. You're growing so much it's visible and I'm proud to call you my friend.*

My parents instilled in me the morals and ethics that make me who I am. They have loved me in their way, and taught me so many valuable lessons. *Steve and Roberta Stoeffler, I hope that you are honored by your daughter. I am blessed to be her.*

Made in the USA
Charleston, SC
18 December 2009